GROW YOUR OWN
IN POTS

GROW YOUR OWN IN POTS

WITH 30 STEP-BY-STEP PROJECTS USING VEGETABLES, FRUIT, AND HERBS

Kay Maguire

Special photography by Steven Wooster

MITCHELL BEAZLEY

To Jo, to Kip and Matilda and to Mum and Dad

Grow Your Own In Pots
Kay Maguire

First published in Great Britain in 2013 by Mitchell Beazley,
an imprint of Octopus Publishing Group Ltd, Endeavour
House, 189 Shaftesbury Avenue, London WC2H 8JY
www.octopusbooks.co.uk

An Hachette UK Company
www.hachette.co.uk

This US edition published in 2013

Distributed in the US by Hachette Book Group, USA
237 Park Avenue, New York, NY 10017, USA

Distributed in Canada by Canadian Manda Group,
165 Dufferin Street, Toronto, Ontario, Canada M6K 3HA
www.octopusbooksusa.com

Design and layout copyright © Octopus Publishing Group
Ltd 2013
Text copyright © Kay Maguire 2013
Text copyright © The Royal Horticultural Society 2013

ISBN 978 1 84533 717 9

Packaged by Griffin Books
Commissioning Editor Helen Griffin
Publisher Alison Starling
Art Director Jonathan Christie
Senior Art Editor Juliette Norsworthy
Designer Lizzie Ballantyne
Copy-editor Joanna Chisholm
Production Controller Lucy Carter
Proofreader Annelise Evans
Indexer Michèle Clarke
R.H.S. Publisher Rae Spencer-Jones
R.H.S. Editor Simon Maughan

Set in Frutiger, Glypha, and Interstate
Printed and bound in China

Contents

The fruit and flowers of a strawberry plant prove that container crops can be as attractive as they are tasty.

There's a homegrown revolution going on...

Try growing your own delicious food

Kay Maguire: "Growing your own makes you happy, healthy, and it's fun too!."

Over the last few years there has been a surge in the popularity of growing your own food, and it's estimated that a quarter of Britons now do so. In many instances this trend has been fuelled by concerns about climate change, rising food costs, "air miles," and the simple desire for fresh, healthy, "real" food.

It's probably no coincidence that this has occurred during a time of global economic crisis. Although growing some of your own food won't solve your financial worries, any gardener will tell you that gardening makes you happy and keeps you sane. Add to that the fun, sense of satisfaction, and utter joy that eating something you have grown yourself brings and it is no wonder so many people are giving it a go.

And I don't believe it's a passing phase. Apart from the fact that the growing-your-own movement has been driven by real need— whether financial, environmental, or a yearning for delicious food—it is also kept going by the interest of gardeners. Once you've dabbled in this hobby there's little inclination to retreat!

I began growing food in the late 1970's, with my Dad on a community garden; and 30 years later we are both still at it. There's just no comparison between the plastic-wrapped fruit and veg on the supermarket shelves and something you have grown from seed, tended, and nurtured against the worst of the weather and munching slugs. The food is fresh, healthy, often free from chemicals and guilt, and tastes amazing.

Pots of herbs and salad leaves are easy to look after and develop quickly, so are great first crops to get you started in growing your own food.

Figs grow almost better in pots than in open ground, because constriction around their roots encourages them to fruit well.

Growing crops in pots gives absolutely everyone the opportunity to have a go. The greatest uptake of grow your own has been in urban areas, with gardeners grabbing what space they can. Cities generally enjoy sheltered microclimates—often sun traps—which are just perfect for growing fruit and vegetables.

Therefore anyone with a windowsill or access to the space on which to stand a few pots can grow a little food. It's the perfect solution if you have very little space, as you can use wall pots, window boxes, and hanging baskets. Even if you have little or no dirt, you can still grow food on a roof terrace, balcony, or deck. As you can see, you don't need a community garden or a large yard—in fact you don't need a yard at all.

Because pots have their own dedicated soil, it is possible to try crops you couldn't otherwise. For example, you can sow carrots in the fine-textured potting mix that they relish, and ignore any surrounding garden soil that may be very stony, or you can enjoy container-grown, lime-hating blueberries in a yard that may have alkaline soil. In a pot you can also confine thuggish, invasive plants such as mint and horseradish, while nursing tender crops such as citrus or grapes, moving them to shelter in winter in cool-temperate areas. Pots are therefore the answer if your yard has difficult or tricky soil for example, if it is boggy or very dry and poor.

Container-grown plants can look great too, creating a striking feature on a deck or by a front

Tomatoes have long been a favorite crop for growing in pots, but these hungry, thirsty plants do need regular care.

Carrots grow really well in containers, where you can give them the perfect, stone-free soil they need.

door. The effect is enhanced when the crop looks particularly attractive. Beans, chard, and rhubarb, for example, all look wonderful, and lettuces come in a wide range of colors and textures. Edible crops can be mixed with containers of ornamentals to stunning effect. You can overcome the problems associated with monoculture, too, by encouraging a host of beneficial insects drawn by an array of enticing flowers.

Grow Your Own In Pots gives you everything you need to know about growing fruit, vegetables, herbs, and other edible plants in pots, from getting started to when to harvest. It includes pot sizes, feeding regimes, and potting mix types, and recommends varieties that fare best in a pot. You can then feel confident to have a go, even

if you have never grown an edible crop before. Fortunately most plants look after themselves provided they are fed and watered regularly. If things do go wrong, you will learn from it and get it right next time. By keeping container-grown plants close to the house, they will be quick to access and easy to care for.

Begin with your absolute favorite food, whether it is strawberries or peas, and then move on to something a little different next year, such as squash, borlotti beans, or bok choy. You will soon discover that growing edible crops is fun and very satisfactory—and might just change your life.

Crops that are grown simply for their edible leaves can create a stunning display, full of varied textures and visual interest, when combined in a carefully chosen container.

Techniques & Tools

Planning ahead for a successful harvest

Before you start, think carefully about what your crops need. Give them the best possible chance with the ideal spot—most require warmth, good light, and shelter. Keep container-grown plants well out of the wind, where they would dry out quickly. If you can, plant them up *in situ*. Pots full of potting mix, even small ones, are heavy.

Make sure your container is large enough for your crop, and remember that the smaller the pot the greater the demand for water and nutrients. Quick, shallow-rooting crops such as salads or strawberries can go in grow bags and hanging baskets. Most crops require a pot at least 12in. (30cm) in depth and width, and fruit trees and crops such as rhubarb and horseradish may need pots as big as 36in. (90cm), if not bigger.

There are hundreds of lovely pots out there, in myriad designs, so consider their size, shape, weight, and material before you choose.

Terra-cotta This is the traditional choice of pot. It looks great and is heavy and stable, which is handy for large, tall crops, although not if they need moving to warmer shelter over winter. Terra-cotta is porous, so dries out quickly

Terra-cotta pots look fantastic, but may need lining with bubble wrap to help in reducing the drying out of potting mix and to insulate plant roots in winter.

and is not frost-proof unless it says so. Glazed terra-cotta is slightly tougher than unglazed.

Plastic and fiber glass As well as being cheap, tough, and retaining water well, these materials are light and the pots comparatively movable.

Metal adds a modern touch or a retro look depending on type. It is tough, light (unless lead), and retains water well. Metal gets cold in winter and hot in summer and will eventually rust, so insulate and protect the insides with cardboard or bubble wrap before planting.

Wood is light and strong, but needs lining with plastic to stop it rotting.

Hanging baskets and window boxes are great for making optimum use of vertical space and can contain a surprisingly large harvest.

Recycled containers Old sinks, bathtubs, olive-oil tins, old boots, wine crates, buckets—the list of usable containers is endless. You can grow crops in just about anything as long as it is big enough and sturdy enough with adequate drainage holes. Drill some yourself if you need to.

Grow bags These cheap alternatives to a pot are perfect for shallow-rooting crops.

Different crops will thrive in all sorts of containers whether traditional wooden troughs, grow bags, or recycled plastic tubs. Just ensure all containers have good drainage holes before planting.

Essential kit for crops in pots

- Pots
- Potting mix
- Drainage material
- Mulching material
- Hand trowel and handfork
- Watering can/hose and waterbreaker
- Pruners
- Stakes, canes, twigs
- Twine
- Temporary row covers or netting
- If you are busy, away a lot, or simply have lots of pots, invest in an automatic or drip irrigation system

Certain crops may benefit from additives to the growing medium. Perlite (center) and vermiculite (right) will both help improve drainage for plants that need a lighter soil.

Always use fresh potting mix when sowing seed or potting up. Recycling old potting mix can be problematic because it often harbors disease.

When planting up pots it is a good idea to add slow-release fertilizer to the potting mix, to help plants once they have used up the original store of nutrients in the potting mix.

A mulch of gravel or pebbles will help to conserve moisture for this herb collection and will also keep water away from their crowns to prevent rotting.

Potting mixes

The very best thing you can do for your crops in pots is provide them with good-quality potting mix. All-purpose, soilless mix is a perfectly good growing medium for most crops, but it does vary in quality, so do not just buy the cheapest. Since it is light and free draining, all-purpose soilless mix dries out quickly and can be difficult to rewet.

If you are growing tall crops or plants for longer than a season, use a soil-based potting mix, which is heavier and more stable than a soilless one and it also holds onto water and nutrients better. Specialist potting mixes are also available, depending on your crop—look out for acidic-soil mix for blueberries and specific citrus potting mix.

And don't be tempted to use ordinary garden soil because it may contain pests and diseases.

You may need to add perlite or horticultural grit to the potting mix to improve drainage. Also mixing in food such as slow-release fertilizer granules, garden compost, or well-rotted organic matter, as well as rootgrow to aid root development, at planting time will give your plants a good start. Water-retaining crystals can stop pots drying out, but don't add so much that the potting mix gets waterlogged.

Old pots are useful inside larger containers to reduce the amount of potting mix needed, making them lighter and cheaper to fill.

Fertilizers

If you did not add slow-release fertilizer when planting, any nutrients contained in potting mix will be exhausted after about six weeks. It is then up to you to feed your plants. You can topdress with dry fertilizer, or use a liquid one. A regular all-purpose feed will improve all your crops, but for maximum fruit you need one that is potassium-rich. Chemical fertilizers such as liquid 5–5–10 are available, while organic feeds, usually made from seaweed or comfrey, are excellent all-rounders. Alternatively you can add comfrey leaves to potting mix at planting time or make your own liquid tea by soaking comfrey leaves in a bucket with water for a few weeks.

Drainage materials

Good drainage is absolutely vital in pots. Water must be able to flow away freely, so make sure you line the bottom of the pot with plenty of drainage material—crocks (broken pieces of terra-cotta pot), stones, gravel, and pieces of Styrofoam packaging are all good. Cover the holes at the bottom of the pot with such drainage materials to stop them getting blocked by plant roots or soil. Raising pots up onto feet, bricks, or blocks of wood also improves drainage and is especially helpful if conditions are wet.

Mulches

Mulch is a key ingredient when growing in pots. It is, quite simply, a layer of anything that sits on the surface of the potting mix. It reduces moisture loss, acts as a barrier against weeds and pests, prevents compaction, and helps to insulate plant roots against cold weather. Mulch can also reflect or absorb light and heat depending on its color. Look out for slate, pebbles, crushed shells, and glass beads. The best type of mulch feeds your crops at the same time. Bark, well-rotted organic matter, homemade compost, and leafmold all provide extra nutrients as they break down.

There is no doubt that edible crops can also look attractive. This sweet pepper easily holds its own with the black-eyed Susan vine (*Thunbergia alata*).

Choosing & buying suitable seeds or plants

Hundreds of crop varieties are specifically selected for container growing. Sometimes called patio varieties, they have been bred to be compact and bushy and include types of peppers, tomatoes, squash, peas, and beans; almost every fruit, vegetable, or herb has at least one container variety. They will certainly give you a good chance of success, but you do not have to grow only these.

Choose varieties that aren't too vigorous, and in cool-temperate areas look for varieties that crop quickly or early—this is important with vegetables such as tomatoes or eggplants that need a long growing season and would otherwise struggle in a short summer outdoors. When choosing fruit trees opt for those on dwarfing rootstocks or they simply won't survive in a pot.

Once you've chosen your varieties, always get the best-quality seed and plants you can. Now is not the point at which you try to cut costs. Organic seed and young plants are widely available, but consider growing heritage varieties too. Most of these have long histories of cultivation, and they are frequently more interesting and tastier than those on general offer. They are also open pollinated, which makes them ideal for seed-saving at the end of the year if you fancy having a go (see p31).

Catch crops & intercrops

All plants grow at different rates, which is good news if you want to make the most of the space in your pots and sow fast-growing crops in otherwise bare patches of soil. Sow intercrops at the same time as slower-growing crops such as beans, parsnips, or onions and harvest them while you wait. Alternatively sow catch crops in spaces that appear as you harvest other crops. You can sow whole rows or just dot in a few seeds as gaps pop up.

- Beet
- Carrots
- Chard
- Lettuce and salad leaves
- Radishes
- Scallions
- Spinach

Radishes are perfect for growing with other crops. They are fast to harvest—ready in as little as six weeks after sowing.

Most crops have at least one variety, and probably more, that will thrive in a container. Included here are purple-leaved basil, variegated oregano, and red-edged lettuce.

When investing in a fruit tree look for a nursery that holds local varieties. A tree that has been bred with your local environment in mind is likely to be happier, healthier, and more successful than any other. Otherwise visit a specialist nursery where you will get specific advice about container growing and the best rootstocks and types of tree.

What can't grow in pots

Sadly a small number of crops are definitely best left in the ground. Perennials such as artichokes are simply too big and greedy for even the largest pots, while a crop such as asparagus, which takes years of patience to bring to harvest, would yield only the smallest of crops in a container, albeit a fine one.

Most brassicas need firm soil to keep them stable and to produce a decent head, something difficult to achieve in a pot, and they are slow growing. If you have any open yard at all grow these beautiful plants there instead.

Always look for strong, healthy plants when buying fruit trees. They are an investment and will be with you for a long time.

How to establish all kinds of crops

If you don't have the time, space, or inclination to grow your crops from seed, or have simply missed the opportunity, young plants are readily available to buy as seedlings, transplants, or larger plants ready to plant out. Although fewer varieties are offered compared to seed, plants are usually ready from spring onwards. You will have more choice if you go to specialist nurseries rather than your local garden center.

If buying tender vegetable plants such as beans and zucchini harden them off before they go out permanently, once the danger of all frosts has passed. Acclimatize them over the course of a week by putting your new plants outside during the day and bringing them indoors overnight so that they gradually get used to the change in temperature and general outdoor conditions. When you finally plant them out, do it in the morning if you can, so they have the whole day to settle in. Make sure you are ready to pot up your new purchases as soon as they arrive, otherwise keep them well watered until you can.

Planting up young plants

1 Water the plants while still in their pots.

2 Line the bottom of the pot with drainage material (see p15) and add potting mix (see p14) to just under the depth of your new plants. Mix in any grit that might be needed for drainage or slow-release fertilizer now.

3 Tease apart the plants' roots if there is more than one plant in the same pot, and plant individually, firming the potting mix in gently as you go. Leave ³⁄₄in. (2cm) between the top of the soil and the pot rim to make watering easier.

4 Mulch with gravel or organic matter, and water the plants in well. Make sure slug and snail control measures are in place (see p32).

Seed sowing directly into pots outdoors

Most crops can be sown directly outside when the time is right, usually as the days get warmer in midspring, and this is easily the simplest, cheapest, and most time efficient way of growing most vegetables and many herbs.

1 Break up any lumps of potting mix with your hands or a hand rake.

Tomatoes, whether sown by you or a nursery, will need growing on indoors before they are ready to go outside.

Most seedlings such as this spinach need thinning so that plants have room to grow well. Overcrowding can lead to weak, disease-prone plants.

2 Water the potting mix—this stops smaller seeds being washed around and helps germination.

3 Mark a furrow, or make holes with a dibble.

4 Sow pinches of seed thinly in the furrow. Drop larger, individual seeds into the holes.

5 Keep the soil moist while seed germinates.

6 Thin out seedlings to give them space to grow well. Thin to their final spacings when they are about 1¼in. (3cm) high.

Starting seed indoors

Some crops such as tomatoes and eggplants need to be sown indoors if your climate does not have the long, warm summers such plants need to germinate, mature, flower, and fruit. By growing such plants from seed you can benefit from the large selection of seed varieties. You will also get a headstart with other more tender crops that cannot be sown outdoors until later in the season, such as beans, zucchini, winter squash, and sweet corn.

Fortunately you don't need much equipment. A propagating unit is handy, although a warm, bright windowsill will do. Any small pot (with drainage holes) including old yogurt pots will work, or make your own from newspaper or toilet-paper roll tubes. Otherwise cell packs with individual cells are well worth investing in—one seed goes in each cell, so no thinning is required, and they are ideal for crops such as cilantro and peas that hate root disturbance.

A warm, sunny windowsill is a good first home for many seedlings and young crops, provided that it is well lit.

1 Fill pots or a cell pack with potting mix and tap down so that it settles.

2 Water the soil with a fine water-breaker.

3 Thinly scatter seed onto the surface of the potting mix or make a shallow hole and push individual seeds into each, following the instructions on the seed packet for sowing depth and germination conditions.

4 Cover the pot or cell pack with plastic wrap or an inverted, clear polyethylene bag, and seal.

5 Place on a warm, light windowsill and keep the potting mix moist while seed germinates.

6 As soon as seedlings appear take off the cover.

7 When the first true leaves develop transfer the seedlings into larger individual pots. When doing this always handle the seedlings by their leaves rather than their stems, and plant each seedling up to its first true leaves.

8 Pot up again, a few weeks later, into larger pots.

9 When frosts have passed, harden plants and then plant out into their final containers.

Planting a fruit tree

Make sure your pot is large enough—your tree will be in there a long time. Go for a pot a couple of sizes bigger than the one it came in; a pot 16in. (40cm) in diameter is a good-sized first one, but remember in a couple of years the tree will need potting up into a bigger container. If you have a bareroot tree, make sure the roots have plenty of room to spread out.

1 Soak trees in water to give them a good drink before planting.

2 Line the bottom of the pot with drainage material (see p15). Add sufficient soil-based potting mix on which to sit the rootball and gauge the depth. You should be able to see the soil mark on the stem, showing at what depth the tree was previously planted.

3 Plant it at this depth, making sure there is a 1 1/4–1 1/2 in. (3–4cm) gap between the surface of the potting mix and the rim of the pot.

This standard peach will need potting up into ever larger pots every few years as it grows, until it is in its final pot of about 24in. (60cm) in diameter.

4 Fill in around the roots with potting mix, firming gently until the tree is sitting snugly in the pot.

5 If your tree needs staking, use a short stake— you only want to secure the roots against the wind, not to stop the whole tree from moving. Knock two thirds of the stake into the potting mix and tie it loosely to the tree.

6 Water in well and mulch.

How to nurture & protect your crops

There is no getting around the fact that plants in pots need more attention than those in the ground. They are living off a limited supply of water and food and are reliant on you to keep that supply topped up. Do so and most of your crops should tick along quite happily, but occasionally plants need a little extra attention—some require pruning or tying in to supports, others may need protection against pests or moving to a sheltered spot.

Whatever the task is it won't be difficult—the beauty of growing in pots is that everything is small scale. Give your crops what they need, and it will make all the difference to the harvests you reap at the end of the season.

Be vigilant. During the summer growing months you need to check your pots every day, sometimes twice, but a quiet stroll in the mornings or with a glass of something in the evenings is a small and surprisingly pleasant price to pay to ensure your crops are in good shape. As well as ensuring you don't miss anything—be it wilting leaves, a munching caterpillar, or a crop that is ready for picking—such a routine will save you time and effort in the long run.

Watering

This will be your main occupation when growing plants in pots; you may as well face that fact right from the start. Never assume that recent rainfall will have done the job for you, especially if pots are sitting in rain shadows cast by a wall or fence. Make life easy for yourself by keeping pots close to a faucet and by investing in a decent hose—ferrying watering cans backward and forward becomes anything but a labor of love after a while, no matter how small your area for containers. Get a spray gun with a water-breaker or fit a water-breaker to your watering can to avoid compacting the soil surface. If you are planning on having lots of container-grown pots invest in a suitable irrigation system.

Feeding

Feeding is almost as important as watering, and different crops all have their own needs. Most plants require a regular feed during the growing and fruiting seasons. Once the nutrients in the potting mix run out—after about six weeks—it is up to you to provide the source of nutrients. One of the easiest ways to remember when to feed your crops is always to do it on the same day of the week. It should then slot neatly into your routine and hopefully you won't ever forget.

Ensuring crops are in good condition

It may seem a bother, but keeping your plants well tended increases yield and makes sure they are in good health. Herbs benefit from regular picking and pinching back of the growing tips to encourage lots of young, bushy growth, while edible flowers need constant deadheading to help more flowers to develop. Support tall plants such as beans, peas, cucumbers, grapes, and trained fruit trees with tepees, obelisks, and bamboo canes, tying them in every now and then to guide them in the right direction. Give fruit trees and bushes at least an annual prune to keep them in shape, promote fruiting, protect them from disease, and extend their lives.

Watering your pots will be your main job in the summer months, with some crops such as tomatoes needing watering every day. Do this early in the day or in the evening.

Regular feeding is vital for strong, healthy, productive plants. Use ready-made fertilizer, diluted if appropriate at the recommended rate, or make your own comfrey tea (see p15).

Mint plants are always best grown on their own in pots rather than with other plants, which they can overwhelm.

Pollinating

A small number of crops benefit if you help them with pollination. Fruit trees such as peaches or plums may be in flower when few pollinators are about; in this case transfer the pollen from flower to flower with a small brush by rubbing gently

Above: Bees are most welcome pollinators, buzzing around flowers like this raspberry in spring and summer.

Left: Place pots together to create a mini microclimate. Plants will provide shade for each other, and humidity is increased.

If insects are lacking in your yard or you are growing on a windy site, help plants such as eggplants by pollinating flowers gently with a small brush.

Protect fruiting plants such as strawberries from the birds with a diamond-mesh netting. Support it on hoops and stretch it tautly across plants so as not to trap birds.

on the stamens. Wind-pollinated corn may need a swift tap to the tassels to help pollen dust the female flowers below. Pollination information can be found where appropriate in the individual directory entries, but some tips include:

chili peppers and sweet peppers—brush flowers carefully (see p83);

eggplants—brush flowers (see p82);

plums—rub blossom with a brush (see p53);

pole beans—mist flowers with water to help them set (see p118);

strawberries—rub flowers gently with a brush (see p70);

tomatoes—shake or mist flowers to transfer pollen (see p76).

Potting up

Every two or three years all perennial plants need transferring into larger pots filled with fresh potting mix. If possible give them the next pot size up, but once they reach the largest size— generally 20–24in. (50–60cm) in diameter—just give their roots a prune before replanting them in fresh potting mix in their previous pot. In the years when potting up is not done give plants a boost by scraping away the top 2in. (5cm) of soil and replacing it with fresh mix every spring.

Providing the optimum growing environment

Having raised strong, healthy plants it is important to nurture them in as helpful an environment as possible. That 2in. (5cm) layer of mulch is a vital weapon in helping your plants grow strongly and healthily so they are more able to resist pests and diseases. It is also a good idea to erect barriers to protect your plants if you suspect problem pests such as birds, insects including caterpillars and beetles, or even hungry mice, are likely to attack (see pp32–5).

An industrial container such as this makes a great raised bed. It is wide and deep enough to grow a whole range of crops.

Above left: Ladybeetles are invaluable in the yard and are one of our main helpers in the war against aphids.

Above right: A bird house will help to attract birds.

Encourage beneficial insects and natural predators into your yard by growing as diverse a range of plants as you can. Mix things up by placing pots of different crops next to each other and plant combinations of crops in larger pots. Growing herbs, flowers, and well-known companion plants with your fruit and veg will attract pollinators such as bees and helpful insects such as ladybeetles, hoverflies, and lacewings (see box opposite). This is much easier to arrange if using pots than in a veg garden, where plants are often grown in rows and blocks of single crops. Think of your pots as a community of plants. Diversity will bring balance and if you can mix in some helpful, beneficial plants then all the better.

Having an area of water nearby, even a tiny one, can also bring in birds and insects, even frogs and toads if you are lucky. A birdbath would help, but a large, glazed pot, filled with water and a couple of aquatic plants, could attract some surprisingly helpful visitors to help tackle any pests.

Companion plants

Certain plants can be grown together so that they benefit each other in some way. Such companion plants are believed to encourage beneficial insects, repel or deter pests by masking the smell of a host plant, or even sacrifice themselves by attracting pests away from a neighboring crop.

Key companion plants

Basil has insect-repelling leaves, which are said to protect tomatoes from aphids.

Borage is said to protect tomatoes from hornworm and is a great pollinator magnet.

Cilantro exudes a scent that is believed to repel aphids and carrot rust fly.

Garlic chives have a powerful smell, which is said to protect carrots from carrot rust fly and can repel aphids from raspberries.

Lavender is a great draw for pollinators and its strong scent is said to confuse pests.

Marigolds (*Tagetes*) are said to deter aphids from beans and whitefly from tomatoes.

Nasturtium is reputed to lure aphids away from beans and brings in beneficial insects.

Protecting against the elements

If plants are struggling in a heatwave, group pots together in the shade. Plants in pots are also much more susceptible to cold than those in the ground, so if hard frosts are forecast insulate plant roots by wrapping pots in bubble wrap or burlap sacking stuffed with straw. Mulching plants also helps to stop roots from freezing. Plunge small pots into the ground if you have the space. Move frost-tender plants to a sheltered spot away from frost pockets, group pots together, and wrap each plant in floating row cover or net-curtain material. In very wet weather move pots under cover and take away any saucers so the plants do not become waterlogged. Raising pots up onto feet or blocks of wood helps excess water drain away.

If you grow some flowering plants with and around your edible crops, they will help to bring in beneficial insects.

Stress-free watering

Watering is one of the most demanding aspects of growing plants in containers. Your crops are in only a finite amount of soil so your watering regime directly affects the quality and amount of food that you get. You need to watch your pots carefully, especially during a hot summer and at particular times, such as when plants are in fruit and require watering every day. However it is possible to make the best use of water without wasting your time or this valuable resource.

There are a number of things you can do that will help to conserve water. First, use the biggest container you can: 12–16in. (30–40cm) or more in diameter and depth is ideal. Plastic pots are much better at retaining water than the more porous, terra-cotta ones, although you can use a sealant or line terra-cotta pots with plastic to improve their water-holding capabilities. Second, use soil-based potting mix for longer-term crops (e.g. fruit) and thirsty ones (e.g. tomatoes); all-purpose soilless mixes, particularly peat-based ones, drain more freely. Third, before planting you could mix in water-retaining crystals to help the potting mix hold onto water for longer, but don't overdo the quantities. Too many crystals can push plants out of their pots and cause waterlogging. Finally, after planting, always mulch the pot. Covering the soil mix with a 2in. (5cm) layer of stone, gravel, or organic matter significantly reduces the amount of moisture lost from the top layer of soil as well as helps to prevent the many problems exacerbated by water loss.

When deciding what to grow it's worth keeping in mind that some crops need more water than others. Leafy veg such as lettuces and fruiting crops such as tomatoes and zucchini require lots of water, while onions, garlic, and shallots demand much less.

Collect and store as much rainwater as you can from your house, carport, and even shed, and help yourself and your plants by installing a drip irrigation system, especially if you have lots of pots. This delivers water exactly where the plants need it, and gradually soaks into the soil so there is no runoff or waste. Such a system will also save time because you will no longer need to carry hoses and watering cans around.

Optimum watering tips

- Check the moisture level in each pot every day during the growing season.
- Don't overwater. Keep the potting mix moist but not soggy and be consistent—don't flood your pots and then subject them to drought. Applying a little water often is best practice.
- Group pots together to create beneficial, mutual shade.
- Always water in the evening or early in the morning so that water reaches plant roots rather than evaporating in the day. Keep in mind however that watering later in the day can attract slugs and snails to vulnerable plants such as seedlings.
- Remove any weeds in your pots at once.
- For very thirsty, deep-rooting plants, such as tomatoes, sink a pot or an upturned plastic bottle with the base cut off into the potting mix near the plant and water directly into it. This helps direct the water straight to where it is needed.

Drip irrigation systems are helpful if you have lots of containers or simply to save the time and worry of watering.

Always collect rainwater where you can in the yard. Having a few water barrels close by will save you carrying watering cans too far between containers.

Watering with a can without a water-breaker helps water to flow down to the roots below.

A good time of day to water is the morning, when strong sun will not cause it to evaporate; it sets plants up for the day.

Harvesting & storing crops

Harvesting is not an exact science. The length of time from sowing to cropping can depend on the variety, the weather, and where you are growing, but if you think something looks ready why not try it and see? Most crops need picking before they go past their best and to keep more produce coming. A few, such as the root vegetables carrots and parsnips and most citrus fruit, can be left in the ground or on the tree until you want them.

Nothing beats the taste of fresh, homegrown produce straight from the yard, and this is definitely the best way to enjoy your crops if you can. But if you find yourself with a glut of something there is no need to waste any of your hard-earned produce. Most fruit, vegetables, and herbs will keep in the refrigerator for a few days. Otherwise almost everything you grow can be frozen, dried, stored, or pickled, depending on the crop. Individual instructions on harvesting and storing are provided in each entry in the crop directories (see pp40–169). If you plan it right you can enjoy something delicious from your pots every month of the year.

Tomatoes will happily stay ripe on the plant until you are ready to pick them, ensuring they are always fresh.

Blueberry fruit ripens at different times so keep checking plants and picking often, to ensure you don't miss any.

How to collect & save seed

Although most seed is inexpensive, the cost does add up, so to make a small financial difference to your outlay every year why not collect and save your own seed? More rewarding than any monetary gain however is the satisfaction you get in completing the circle—from crop to seed to crop again. You can also exchange seed with friends and family or get involved in some of the organized seed swaps that take place within state and federal horticultural groups and community gardens.

Some results from home-collected seed won't be quite as predictable as they would be with store-bought seed: for example, seed from F_1 hybrids can be tricky and it's a gamble to know what sort of crop you will get—if any at all. Seed from heritage varieties and other hybrids is much more reliable and worth collecting. Easy seeds to save include beans, peas, winter and summer squash, tomatoes, cilantro, fennel, and lettuces that have bolted.

- On a dry day collect seed—only from healthy plants.
- Remove the whole seedhead and place it in a paper bag.
- Dry it in a heated cabinet or on a windowsill before extracting the seed.
- Remove any remaining chaff from the seed, then store it somewhere cool and dry in an airtight jar. The refrigerator is better than a kitchen cupboard.
- Always label and date the seed.
- Clean seed from fleshy fruit such as tomatoes by sifting the fruit and then rinsing the pulp from the seed. Leave to dry before storing.

Right: When picking beans late in the season, leave a few on the plant to dry. Collect them for their seed before the frost.

Cut off whole seedheads of cilantro. Put them in paper bags to dry, before rubbing off and storing the seeds.

Solving common problems

Growing in containers presents a unique set of challenges: You are raising plants in a limited space and have to take extra care with watering and feeding. If you get this right you will have strong, healthy, productive plants that are less vulnerable to attack and more able to stand up for themselves if attacks are made.

Always give crops the space they need; do not be tempted to overcrowd your pots in such limited growing conditions. Keep on top of the watering routine, but do not overdo it—waterlogging can cause its own troubles. Remember to feed your crops once a week during the growing season. A 2in. (5cm) layer of mulch will help your plants to grow strongly and healthily.

Slugs and snails can devastate seedlings and young plants so ensure the plants are adequately protected at all times.

Once you have mastered these cultural tactics, use any other precautionary measures you can to protect your plants. Barrier deterrents such as netting and floating row cover make an enormous difference, as does squashing or picking off insect pests such as caterpillars, aphids, slugs, and snails as soon as you spot them. Lay wire poultry fencing or prickly-leaved plants such as holly over containers of newly sown seed or recently germinated plants to deter squirrels and mice. A few chemical treatments are available, but they can have a detrimental effect on the ecosystem of your yard, so never apply such chemicals when plants are in flower. Note the instructions for use of the pesticide, particularly on the period that must be left between treatment and harvesting.

It is impossible and therefore pointless to try to be free of all pest and disease problems in the yard; they are an inevitable and necessary part of the ecosystem. Fortunately the main culprits you will encounter are fairly predictable, so be vigilant, spot them early, and try to keep their numbers and damage to a minimum.

Slugs and snails will definitely be your most frustrating troublemakers, and the best form of defence is to try everything. Always be on the lookout for slugs and snails, and if they're getting out of hand a twilight collecting prowl can work wonders. Slug pellets, containing ferric phosphate, scattered thinly around vulnerable

Right: Covering the potting mix around vulnerable plants and seedlings with a thick layer of sharp grit or gravel should help in the battle against slugs and snails.

More slug & snail controls

- **Copper tape** gives slugs and snails an electric shock and is ideal for wrapping around the rim of each pot. Or try smearing each rim with petroleum jelly.
- **Beer traps** Sink an old jelly jar or yogurt pot into the soil and fill it with beer.
- **Nematodes** are natural predators that can be watered into the soil when temperatures are above 41°F (5°C).
- **Grit, gravel, crushed eggshells, or crushed seashells** Spread a thick layer of anything sharp and gritty inside the rim of the pot, between rows of seedlings, or as a mulch.
- **Citrus skins** Lay pieces of citrus-fruit rind from oranges and grapefruit face up on the surface of the potting mix around vulnerable plants. Simply check each morning and dispose of the slugs.

plants are an effective form of control; other pellet types are more toxic to children, pets, and wildlife. Further ideas are given in the checklist (see box above). If you use traps, dispose of your prisoners by dissolving them in salty water, by snipping them in half with pruners, or by putting them in a bag in the trash can.

Remove snails immediately whenever you see them. This is more effective at night when they are at their most active.

Powdery mildew is the white mold that appears on both the upper and lower surfaces of leaves in dry weather. It is worse where there is poor air circulation among plants, so don't overcrowd your pots. Mulching and consistent watering will reduce stress. Look out for resistant cultivars in seed catalogs

Aphids, including blackfly and greenfly, love soft, new growth so are mainly a problem in spring, even though they are around until late summer. They will not kill your plants, but they can weaken them and also spread viruses and other diseases. Ladybeetles, hoverflies, and lacewings are their natural predators, so encourage these into your yard. Aphids can also be rubbed off by hand, which is effective if there are only a few plants to treat. They can also be hosed off with insecticidal soap.

Attracting beneficial insects such as ladybeetles, hoverflies, and lacewings will help to reduce aphids on your plants.

Late blight is the disease most vegetable gardeners dread. This airborne fungal disease, which is common in the moist, warm conditions of late summer, affects tomatoes and potatoes and can attack the whole plant, destroying a crop very quickly. Look out for chocolate-brown blotches on the leaves and stems, which will eventually spread to the fruit or tubers and the whole plant will become slimy and black. Be vigilant and remove infected leaves immediately, although it is only a matter of time before it takes hold. Cut the stems of potatoes down to the soil surface at once, crossing your fingers it hasn't spread to the potatoes below. Wait a couple of weeks before lifting your potatoes, to allow the skins to thicken. As soon as you spot signs of late blight, pick all your tomatoes, ripe or not. When plants are infected don't compost them, but put them in bags and trash them. Resistant varieties are also available—try the 'Sarpo' range of potatoes and 'Ferline' or 'Legend' tomatoes.

Caterpillars of the cabbage white butterflies love all brassicas, such as cabbages, as well as radishes, so if you are growing these it is best to be prepared by netting the plants. Otherwise, as soon as you see the butterflies flitting round your pots, look for the eggs and squash them. Their caterpillars will be on the munch from late spring until the fall.

Beetles such as the stripy rosemary beetle love anything in the rosemary family and also eat the leaves of lavender and sage. Adults feed during late summer, and the larvae can be found on the undersides of leaves from the fall to spring. Tap them onto newspaper laid around your pots or pick them off by hand.

Flea beetles are a problem on all young brassicas, including radishes, Oriental leaves, cabbages, and arugula, peppering their leaves with holes. Damage is often worse in warm, dry weather. You may avoid attacks by growing crops in tall pots, which these flying insects cannot

Keep an eye out for the telltale signs of late blight from midsummer onward and particularly after rain.

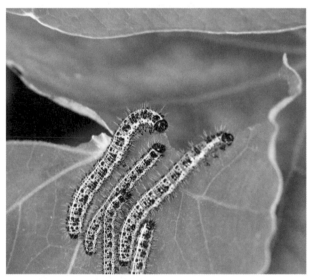

Caterpillars of the cabbage white butterfly can ruin your crop unless you cover plants with a mesh netting to stop the butterflies laying eggs on the leaves.

reach, or by covering seedlings with netting to keep the flea beetles away. If plants are attacked, paint a piece of cardboard with something sticky such as molasses or syrup. Wave it across or above the leaves, and the beetles jump off the leaves onto the cardboard, which you then discard.

By following a few simple steps and putting some useful cultural principles into practice even seasoned vegetable growers will be surprised at how much produce they can get from such a small area.

Square-yard, year-round planter

Growing your own vegetables doesn't have to be all about space. It is perfectly possible to concentrate on just a single planter 3 x 3ft. (1 x 1m) and, by growing intensively and making constant use of all the space, get a fantastic yield with minimal effort.

Based on the Square Foot gardening concept, this idea uses small areas of land for intensive vegetable growing and is ideal for large containers or square raised beds—but it doesn't even need to be a perfect square or exactly 3 x 3ft. (1 x 1m). By sowing crops closer than you normally would and immediately replacing each crop with a different one as soon as it's harvested, you can enjoy maximum yield in the minimum time and space. Such concentrated growing

means there are fewer gaps for weeds to colonize and the intensive plant coverage acts as a living mulch, helping to retain water and prevent weeds. Thus maintenance tasks are quicker and easier than with a large site.

You can grow absolutely anything, but why not try a simple selection of catch crops of leaves (for example, bok choy, lettuces, spinach), beet, carrots, scallions, and radishes with zucchini, a row of beans, and a tomato plant inside a raised bed of 3 x 3ft. (1 x 1m)?

You do need a patch of ground for this project, as well as sufficient room around it to reach across the bed to sow, weed, water, and harvest, so you can avoid walking on the soil.

The raised bed should be in a sunny spot so that it gets maximum light. Fill it with the best soil you can get, mixing in plenty of garden compost or well-rotted organic matter. It's a good idea to add slow-release fertilizer too, to give your crops the best possible start. After this initial preparation the bed is not dug again, thus helping to preserve the soil structure and also entailing less work.

Spacing and sowing crops

Seed is spot sown where possible, which means that you sow at the correct final spacings and don't spend time thinning out later. You also plant in squares, not rows, giving equal space between individual plants; thus they can be grown closer than normal. When using miniature or compact varieties you can plant even closer and get a greater yield, even if the crops are sometimes of a smaller size. The number of plants grown in each square depends on the crop, and some crops may occupy more than one square. In one square for example you can grow: 16 beets or carrots; or six spinach plants; or two beans; but only a single zucchini. Some larger plants, such as zucchini, will eventually take up more than one square, but in the meantime use the surrounding squares for faster-growing crops such as radishes or salad leaves.

Start sowing in spring with early, fast-growing crops in each square. These can be harvested in time for a second sowing, by which time it's safe to sow more tender plants such as zucchini. Make the best use of space by growing plants that climb up supports: beans, peas, tomatoes, squash, cucumbers, even some types of zucchini can all be grown vertically. Just make sure that

SQUARE-YARD CHECKLIST

- This technique is suitable for practically all crops. Just keep in mind that some of them, such as onions, are in the ground for a long time, while others, such as brassicas, occupy a lot of space.
- Plant bushy crops such as sweet peppers and some types of zucchini at the corners so they do not take over the bed.
- Although the raised bed requires regular attention, maintenance is minimal. When tackled a square at a time, the tending of such small spaces takes minutes rather than hours, and the intensive culture creates a microclimate that conserves moisture and keeps weeds down.
- Add garden compost and slow-release fertilizer at every harvest so you are amending the soil throughout the season.
- Extending the season is simple. Either warm the whole bed with black landscape fabric in early spring before sowing or concentrate on individual squares by placing temporary row covers just where they are needed. Floating row cover can be laid over late crops to protect them against cold weather.

you plant them at the northern end of your bed so that shade is cast away from the rest of the crops. If there is space add in some companion plants (see p27).

Optimal use

Once a crop is harvested, clear it away and sprinkle in slow-release fertilizer at the same time as digging fresh garden compost or manure into its square. Then sow a new crop. This makes optimum use of each space by never leaving any patches of bare soil idle. It also means you are constantly amending the soil in the raised bed.

Planting your square-yard, year-round planter

What you need

- raised bed, 3 x 3ft. (1 x 1m); ■ garden soil or soil-based potting mix; ■ garden compost; ■ measuring tape; ■ hammer, nails; ■ garden twine; ■ vegetable seeds (see p36); ■ bamboo canes; ■ indeterminate tomato plant

1 Fill the raised bed with two parts garden soil and one part garden compost mixed together. Using the measuring tape divide the raised bed into a grid of evenly sized squares; this bed has 16 squares of 10 x 10in. (25 x 25cm). Tap in nails at each point.

2 Run the garden twine between the marker nails across the bed and knot each end tightly once it is taut. Then water the bed using a hose or watering can with a water-breaker so it is ready for sowing.

6 Harvest your crops when they are ready. As each square empties, fork a trowelful of fresh garden compost and some slow-release fertilizer into it and resow. These radishes were in and out before the zucchini required more room to grow.

7 Once all frosts have passed other more tender crops can be sown. Allocate four squares in a corner for a single zucchini, sowing it in the corner square to give the plant maximum space to spread out. This is a patio variety, which worked particularly well here.

8 Make a framework of bamboo canes for your beans and sow a row along the three squares at the back of the raised bed, saving the fourth square for the indeterminate tomato.

3 Before sowing your first crops work out the appropriate number of seeds for each crop in its allocated square—one, four, six, nine, or 16 seeds may fit in the square, depending on the crop. Then make sure that each seed is evenly spaced within the square.

4 Water in the seeds well. A watering can with a water-breaker is perfect for this because you can concentrate on each square one at a time as necessary.

5 If slugs and snails are a problem (see p32) try to deter them for example by sticking a strip of copper tape around the rim of the raised bed. Both slugs and snails hate the feel of it and should leave your precious plants alone. Feed and water the plants regularly.

9 Plant an indeterminate tomato in its allocated square and tie it to its own cane for support. Continue tying in and pinching back sideshoots on the tomato throughout summer.

10 You can add some companion plants at the corners and around the tomato. This may help to bring in pollinating insects for your flowering crops and encourage ladybeetles, which feed on pests such as aphids that can damage crops.

11 Keep harvesting your crops as soon as they are ready. Depending on the crops you can keep refreshing the soil and resowing well into summer, and you should then still be harvesting right up until the first frosts.

Fruit

Apples

Thanks to dwarf rootstocks apple trees fare very happily in containers—you do not need an orchard to harvest your own sweet, crisp apples. There are hundreds of different varieties so the first thing you need to decide is whether you want to eat the apples or cook with them. If you have the space why not try both, but make sure your chosen varieties flower at the same time so they can pollinate each other. If you want to grow only one tree, select a variety that is self fertile or try a family tree—one that has two or more varieties grafted onto the trunk, giving you a different apple on each main branch.

Basic needs
Use a pot 18–20in. (45–50cm) in diameter with soil-based potting mix combined with grit. Half-barrels are good.

Growing techniques
1 Look for a named cultivar that has been specially grown for a container and has been grafted onto 'M26' or 'M9' rootstock (see p44).

2 Plant bareroot trees in the dormant season between the fall and late winter; container-grown plants can be planted at any time. Water well and place in a warm, sheltered site.

3 Work rootgrow or all-purpose fertilizer such as alfalfa meal into the planting hole. Stake the tree (see pp44–5). Then mulch.

4 Keep an eye on watering, particularly in dry spells and when the fruit starts to swell.

An apple tree can be grown as a single-stem cordon where space is limited.

If growing apples in a frost-prone area choose later-flowering varieties to prevent frost damage.

5 From spring onward feed every two weeks with an all-purpose liquid feed.

6 Topdress in winter with manure.

Problem solving
Apples are susceptible to damage from codling moths. They also suffer from fungal diseases such as apple scab, where damage is generally only skin deep and can be peeled away. Some varieties offer resistance to apple scab. Wet summers cause brown rot: discard infected fruit when you see it. Erratic watering can cause sunken holes in fruit, known as bitter pit; fortunately affected fruit can still be eaten.

Harvesting and storage
Windfalls on the ground or in the container are a good sign fruit is ripe. Pick by cupping an apple and twisting it on its stem—there should

be no need to pull. Different varieties are ready at different times, and if you choose your trees carefully you can harvest over a long period. Early varieties are ready from midsummer and must be eaten fairly quickly as they do not store well. Others are harvested in midfall, and these can be stored in a cool basement or shed. When storing apples do not let them touch, and check regularly for spoiling and rotting. Apples can also be puréed and frozen, or slow dried in the oven before storing.

VARIETIES cooking: 'Arthur Turner', 'Emneth Early'; eating: 'Discovery', 'Pixie', 'Sunset'

Expert tips

- Plant a pot-grown tree at the same depth as previously. If a bareroot tree, look for the soil mark on the stem (see p45).

- Pot up every other year in the fall, cutting off any thick roots. Once in its final pot, refresh potting mix every year, giving the tree a root prune every alternate year.

- Unless you choose a self-fertile variety or family tree, you need to grow more than one tree. Trees are grouped according to pollination so grow trees in the same or adjoining group. Seek advice from a specialist nursery when buying.

- Pruning depends on the way your tree has been trained and where it fruits—either on branch spurs or tips. Minarettes (single, vertical-stemmed cordons) are ideal for containers, taking up little room and needing minimal pruning. It is simplest to buy a tree already trained to shape; the main leader can be reduced in spring, if necessary, and new side branches pruned back to three leaves in summer. Thin the stems while the tree is dormant in winter to maintain the formative shape and to keep an open branch structure.

Early apples can be eaten straight from the tree, while later cropping varieties will benefit from storage first.

Apple harvest

Apples are the most popular fruit tree grown and on the right rootstock will thrive in a pot. A simple, single-stemmed cordon looks stunning laden with sweet, refreshing fruit and takes up very little space, so is perfect for a small yard or deck. There are hundreds of varieties to choose from, but go for one that is not readily available in the stores or, even better, buy one that has some sort of historical connection to your area.

When selecting any fruit tree it is important that you consider its rootstock, but when growing in containers the rootstock choice is absolutely vital. You need an 'M26' or 'M9' rootstock. Do not go for the very dwarfing rootstocks; although they are small, growing them in a container puts them under even more stress. Having settled on your choice of rootstock you then need to decide which apple variety you want to grow (see p43). This can be a little tricky if you want only one tree, as it must be self fertile (see p42).

Bareroot and container-grown plants can be planted at different times of year (see p42). Give trees a sunny, sheltered spot so that fruit has the maximum chance of growing and ripening.

Staking will help to anchor the roots and stop windrock. Use a stake that is only one third the height of the tree so that the stem can still sway in the wind and gradually thicken. Insert the stake on the side of the prevailing wind so the tree is blown away from the stake. Make sure the stake is firmly in the potting mix or else it will not anchor the tree. Check the tree tie regularly to make sure that it is not too tight, and loosen it as the tree trunk expands.

Keep your tree well watered in dry weather and when the fruit begins to swell. A good mulch will help it to retain moisture as will topdressing the tree with garden compost or well-rotted manure every spring. Water plants regularly with an all-purpose liquid fertilizer.

An apple tree is an investment for the future, and although it may take a little while for your tree to reach full productivity it will be well worth the wait.

Planting your apple tree

What you need
- bareroot apple tree;
- terra-cotta pot at least 16in. (40cm) wide and deep;
- horticultural grit;
- soil-based potting mix;
- fertilizer (see p15);
- stake and tree tie.

1 Unpack your apple tree as soon as it arrives. Place it in a bucket of water so the roots do not dry out. At potting time take a good look at your tree to establish exactly where the graft union is—it is the swollen part where the variety has been joined to the rootstock. This must be well above the surface of the soil after planting.

2 Put a layer of drainage material in the bottom of the pot and then half fill it with potting mix. Mix in some fertilizer and place the tree on top. Insert the stake carefully in-between the roots before filling in with more potting mix. Keep adding mix, firming it down as you go until the tree is stable and the graft union is still above the soil level.

3 Secure the stake to the tree with the tree tie, placing a spacer between the tree stem and the stake to stop them rubbing against each other.

4 Water the tree in well and then mulch with well-rotted manure or garden compost. Top up the mulch if the level drops after watering. Feed and water regularly.

5 Warm weather will encourage your tree to blossom. If hard frosts are forecast, protect the flowers and very young fruit to ensure you still get a good crop.

Pears

Although pears are a little tricky to grow, the taste of homegrown fruit is a world away from what we have become accustomed to from the supermarket. If you are short on space, try a family pear tree, which has two or more varieties grafted onto the trunk, or choose one of the self-fertile varieties, although these do even better when grown with a compatible partner. Always go for the dwarf container rootstock 'Quince C' when growing in pots.

Basic needs
Use a pot 18–20in. (45–50cm) in diameter with soil-based potting mix combined with grit.

Growing techniques
1 In the fall plant at the same level that the tree was in the previous pot or in the ground.

2 Water well, then place the pot in a sunny, sheltered site, well away from any frost pockets.

3 Refresh the top layer of potting mix in spring, sprinkling in slow-release fertilizer and mulching with well-rotted manure. Keep the mulch away from the trunk.

4 Feed once a week in the growing season with an all-purpose liquid fertilizer.

5 Water well in dry weather and as fruit swells.

6 Prune every year in winter and summer.

Expert tips

- For an early crop buy a three-year-old tree.
- Almost all pears are spur fruiting and can be grown as standards or trained as cordons or espaliers. Prune single cordons by reducing the main leader in spring, then prune side branches to three leaves in midsummer, and thin fruiting stems to 4in. (10cm) apart in winter.

For the best-sized fruits thin pears in summer back to two or three fruit per cluster.

Problem solving
Disease resistance in individual cultivars may differ, but always look out for brown rot, particularly in wet summers. Prune out any infected fruit to prevent it spreading. The common pear leaf blister mite causes black blisters on leaves but is mainly cosmetic.

Harvesting and storage
Pears are ready for harvesting when they are firm but have changed color slightly; they should come off the tree with a gentle lift and twist. If gathered too early they will not ripen; if too late they can rot or taste gritty. After picking store pears in a cool, dark place until ripe. Early cultivars take a week to ripen; later ones a few months.

VARIETIES 'Beth', 'Beurré Hardy', 'Catillac', 'Concorde', 'Conference', 'Doyenne du Comice'

Figs

Figs are possibly the perfect crop for growing in pots, because they love having their growth kept in check. Beautifully architectural, with stunning foliage, they make lovely features on a deck or patio. In cool-temperate areas just make sure you choose one of the hardier cultivars to ensure you get a good crop.

Basic needs

Use a pot 14–16in. (35–40cm) in diameter filled with nutrient-rich, soil-based potting mix combined with grit so it drains freely.

This large fig may ripen during summer; the small figs won't, nor will they survive winter. The figs that do overwinter are tiny, and even they may not develop if it is very cold.

Growing techniques

1 Position figs against the warmest, sunniest wall you have to maximize the available heat and light.

2 Keep well watered so the soil never dries out.

3 Mulch in spring with well-rotted organic matter. In summer apply liquid fertilizer every week.

4 In cool-temperate climates move the fig to a frost-free place for the winter. Otherwise insulate the pot with bubble wrap or floating row cover.

5 Pot up every couple of years in spring.

Problem solving

Net plants against birds.

Harvesting and storage

You can smell when figs are ready. They are fragrant and soft to handle, but the longer you wait the sweeter your figs will be. Hold the fruit by the stalk and pull it gently away from the stem. Eat fresh or slowly dry them in the oven.

VARIETIES 'Brown Turkey', 'Brunswick', 'Petite Nigra', 'White Ischia', 'White Marseilles'

Citrus

All members of the citrus family—lemons, limes, grapefruits, kumquats, oranges, and calamondins—are frost tender and need consistently warm temperatures. In cool-temperate regions, grow citrus in a sunroom. Choose light, plastic rather than heavier, clay pots to make this annual task easier. Getting growing conditions right is vital, but other than this citrus plants are really not difficult fruit to grow. They are beautiful, small trees with fragrant flowers blossoming throughout the year, and there is something special about picking your own lemons or oranges that makes any extra effort entirely worthwhile.

Basic needs

Pick a pot 20in. (50cm) or more in diameter for a two- to three-year-old plant. Mix 20 percent grit or sharp sand into soil-based potting mix or use a specialist citrus potting mix. Use acidic-soil mix if you live in a hard-water area and cannot water with rainwater.

Growing techniques

1 For plants to fruit well, the right conditions are key. Citrus needs a long, hot, humid growing season, with at least six months at 59°F (15°C) for fruit to ripen, and a frost-free winter with minimum temperatures of 55°F (13°C). Plants become dormant in temperatures lower than this; and if below 45°F (7°C) they may die.

2 To increase the chances of fruiting, purchase mature plants, because citrus is extremely slow to grow from cuttings or seed.

3 Plant citrus trees in spring.

4 Water well, keeping the potting mix moist, because a lack of water can cause fruit to drop. Rainwater is best if you can collect it. Keep plants almost dry in winter and then as temperatures

In hot, dry summers mist around plants during and after flowering to help increase humidity.

Between the various types, citrus can be found in flower almost year-round. It takes up to a year for fruit to ripen.

Expert tips

- Citrus needs minimal pruning, especially if you are growing dwarf, container varieties. Remove shoots below the graft union on the main stem and pinch back the tips of vigorous growth in summer. In late winter reshape plants by thinning out any overcrowded branches and cutting back leggy branches by two thirds. Beware savage thorns.
- Stand pots on saucers of wet gravel to raise humidity levels. Misting leaves in summer also helps.
- The warmer the temperature the better the fruit tastes.

Citrus grown in pots should be placed in a warm, sunny spot in summer and then, in cool-temperate areas, moved into a frost-free environment to overwinter.

begin to warm up start watering with tepid water to encourage flowering. Allow excess water to drain away so the plant does not sit in it.

5 Refresh the top 2in. (5cm) of potting mix in spring. Every three or four years repot in spring when the roots become congested.

6 Citrus are hungry plants, so feed them throughout the year. From early spring to midfall give plants high-nitrogen fertilizer followed by an all-purpose winter feed. Specialist citrus feeds are also available.

Problem solving

Most problems such as failing to flower, losing flowers early, yellow leaves, or leaf drop are caused by giving plants the wrong conditions. Insufficient light, food, water, or humidity and too low temperatures can all cause problems, so take care not to overwater in winter, avoid fluctuating temperatures, and keep humidity levels high.

Harvesting and storage

Fruit can be picked when ripe or left on the tree. Cut them off with pruners leaving a short stalk. Undamaged fruit can be stored somewhere cool and dry for several weeks, made into preserves, or can be bottled.

VARIETIES clementine: *C. reticulata* Mandarin Group 'Nules'; grapefruit: *C. x paradisi* 'Marsh'; lemon: *C. x meyeri* 'Meyer', *C. limon* 'Garey's Eureka'; orange: *C. sinensis* 'Washington'; Persian lime: *C. aurantiifolia* 'Tahiti'; satsuma: *C. unshiu* 'Owari'

Cherries

Cherries are stunning fruit trees. Dripping blossom in spring then dangling fruit in summer they often end the season with vibrant fall color. There are two types of cherry—sweet or sour. Sweet cherries are best eaten fresh, while sour cherries need cooking before they become delicious enough to eat. All sour cherries are self fertile, but some sweet cherries are not; in these cases seek advice from a specialist nursery to ensure you buy varieties that can pollinate each other. Select dwarfing rootstocks to keep trees at a manageable height of 6½–10ft. (2–3m). 'Table' is a perfect rootstock for sweet cherries in pots, 'Colt' for the less vigorous sour. Grow as bushes or fan train.

Protect cherry blossom against frost with floating row cover but be sure to remove it in the day for foraging bees.

Basic needs
Give trees a large pot, 2ft. (60cm) or more wide, filled with soil-based potting mix.

Growing techniques
1 Plant as bareroot or container plants between late fall and early spring. Sweet cherries need full sun; sour cherries tolerate more shade.

2 Cherries are shallow-rooting and will dry out quickly in pots so water trees well after planting. Watering is also especially important while fruit is first growing and during dry periods.

3 Refresh the top layer of potting mix every spring, sprinkling in an all-purpose, slow-release fertilizer. Give all-purpose liquid feed in summer.

4 Blossom comes early in the season so place the pot in a sheltered site. Protect flowers and fruit from frost with floating row cover; remove the cover to allow access to pollinating insects.

Problem solving
Bacterial canker, seen as brown spots on leaves and the eventual dieback of branches, can kill, so cut out any affected branches and use a copper-based fungicide in late summer. Reduce the chances of silver leaf by pruning in summer. Protect the ripe fruit from birds with netting.

Harvesting and storage
From midsummer onwards, pick cherries by their stalks. Sweet cherries are best eaten when fresh but will keep in the refrigerator for a week. Sour cherries need cooking. Cherries can also be frozen whole (removing stones first) or puréed.

VARIETIES sour: 'Meteor', 'Morello', 'Nabella'; sweet: 'Merchant', 'Stella', 'Summer Sun'

Expert tips

- Sweet cherries fruit on one- and two-year-old stems. Shorten new shoots in summer to encourage the fruiting spurs.

- Sour cherries fruit on wood formed the previous year. Prune out whole shoots in summer to reduce overcrowding and stimulate new growth.

Peaches

A homegrown peach picked fresh from the tree has a taste delectably different from any others you will have tasted. Unfortunately all that taste and evocative aroma need a bit of effort, especially in cool-temperate climates. Peach trees are hardy, but their flowers are not. Go for genetically dwarf, compact types, known as patio peaches, or any conventional type grown on a container rootstock such as 'Pixy' or 'St Julien A.' These are easier to tend.

Peaches don't all mature at once, so keep checking the tree for ripened fruit to pick.

Basic needs
Start young trees in a 8in. (20cm) pot filled with soil-based potting mix combined with grit.

Growing techniques
1 Plant either bareroot or container-grown plants in the fall, placing them against a warm, sunny, sheltered wall. Water them very well.

2 As blossom appears feed with all-purpose liquid fertilizer every couple of weeks. Water regularly.

3 Give the developing fruit room to grow by gradually thinning them out to 2in. (5cm) apart.

4 In spring refresh the potting mix and mulch.

5 Repot every other year into a larger pot. A final pot of 16in. (40cm) diameter should be sufficient.

Problem solving
Peach leaf curl is a common fungal disease that distorts leaves with vivid, pink blisters. It is spread by rain splash, so cover containers between

midwinter and late spring. 'Avalon Pride' is reputed to be resistant to this disease.

In cool-temperate areas cover peach blossom with floating row cover to protect it against frost.

Harvesting and storage
Fruit is ripe when perfumed and soft; pick it regularly. Eat fresh or make into jelly or chutney.

VARIETIES 'Avalon Pride', 'Bonanza', 'Duke of York', 'Garden Annie', 'Garden Lady', 'Peregrine', 'Red Haven', 'Rochester'

Expert tips

- If growing in a cool-temperate climate choose cultivars that flower late or use floating row cover to protect flowers from frost by night; remove the covering by day to allow access to pollinators.

- Increase fruiting potential by pollinating plants yourself with a soft brush.

- Peaches flower on the previous year's growth so need replacement pruning to produce new wood every year. Prune out old shoots to a narrow growth bud. Compact types need little pruning—just cut out dead, diseased, or damaged wood.

- To prevent silver leaf and canker prune only on a dry, sunny day in spring or summer.

Plums

Grow your own and you get to choose between plums, damsons, gages, or bullaces, or plant one of each. They are close relatives, although damsons and bullaces have smaller, tarter fruit that tastes better cooked. There are many self-fertile varieties, but you will have a better crop if you grow two trees from the same or adjacent pollination groups. Go for plants grafted onto the semidwarfing 'Pixy' rootstock and train them as open bushes, pyramids, or fans if they have not already been grown in that shape.

Basic needs
Use a 24in. (60cm) pot with plenty of drainage holes—plums hate sitting in wet soil. Fill it with soil-based potting mix combined with grit.

Growing techniques
1 Plant as bareroot or pot-grown plants in midfall, ensuring trees are inserted at the same level as in the previous pot or ground. Water well.

2 Position the pot in a warm, sunny spot.

3 Plums are thirsty trees, so water well in the first year while they establish; also water in dry spells.

4 Give pots a mulch with well-rotted manure every spring to retain moisture. Feed regularly.

5 Plums are early flowering and although the trees are hardy the flowers are not. Be ready to protect flowers and fruit on frosty nights, removing the cover for pollinators the next day.

6 Improve yields by thinning plums to 3in. (7.5cm) apart when they are small.

Problem solving
Keep pruning to a minimum to avoid silver leaf and bacterial canker; when necessary prune in spring or midsummer. Wasps and birds can be a nuisance so net trees and hang wasp traps. Fruit can also be attacked by maggots of the plum moth or sawfly moth. Erect pheromone traps or spray with a pesticide containing deltamethrin or lambda-cyhalothrin.

Harvesting and storage
All taste best if left to ripen on the tree. Fruit is ready when colored and emitting a sweet, heavy scent. Windfalls are also a good clue. Eat fresh or de-stone and freeze whole or puréed, or make into jelly, chutney, or wine.

VARIETIES bullace: 'Shepherd's Bullace'; damson: 'Farleigh Damson'; gage: 'Cambridge Gage'; plum: 'Blue Tit', 'Opal', 'Victoria'

Mature plum fruit has a distinctive dusty coating, or bloom, that can be rubbed off easily with your fingers.

Olives

As olive trees are evocative for some people of summer vacations and lazy days, having your own tree can be immensely satisfying, particularly if it produces fruit. These slow-growing trees have excellent ornamental properties and in a warm, sheltered position, or in a warm-temperate climate, established trees may produce a crop of olives.

Basic needs
Good drainage is vital so add grit to soil-based potting mix. Start off young olive trees in a 12–14in. (30–35cm) pot.

Growing techniques
1 Grow from young plants, planted in the fall in a sheltered, sunny spot—against a warm house wall is ideal. Stake each tree firmly and water well.

2 Although olives are drought tolerant, you must still water regularly, ensuring the potting mix

By growing more than one cultivar of olive you can greatly improve the yield.

is moist in dry spells. Reduce watering during winter, but do not allow the soil to dry out because it will inhibit flowering later on.

3 Apply an all-purpose liquid feed monthly during the growing season.

Problem solving
Prolonged exposure to the cold can cause splitting bark, dieback, and leaf drop. Plants should regrow, but crops and growth will be affected that season. Scale insects can sometimes be a problem, but this is mainly a cosmetic one. Wipe them off as soon as they are discovered.

Harvesting and storage
Olives can be picked when firm and black and eaten raw, although they won't taste like the store-bought ones you are used to (these are dehydrated in salt and stored in olive oil or brine).

VARIETIES 'Africana', 'Aglandau', 'Cailletier', 'El Greco', 'Frantoio', 'Mission', 'Sativa'

Expert tips

- Olives require little pruning; just thin out branches in spring to keep an open center and prune the tips of the main branches every year after flowering to strong replacement shoots.

- Although most olive trees are self fertile growing more than one cultivar will help pollination and give a more reliable yield.

- Thin out crops to three or four fruit every 12in. (30cm) to help them ripen well and avoid early fruit drop.

- Protect plant roots from frosts in cool-temperate areas by insulating pots with floating row cover or bubble wrap and straw. Trees will be damaged by temperatures below 14°F (-10°C).

Gooseberries

Now undergoing something of resurgence in popularity, gooseberries are old-fashioned fruit with a sweet, sharp punch. They are hardy, easy, and self fertile so you need grow only one plant if space is limited. Gooseberries are available as bushes or trained as cordons or standards, which are perfect for containers because they are very productive but take up little space.

Basic needs

Soil-based potting mix provides stability and water retention. Add some grit, for good drainage, in a pot 12in. (30cm) or more deep.

Growing techniques

1 Plant as bareroot or container-grown plants between late fall and early spring, in a sheltered, sunny spot, although plants still fruit—just less—in shade. Water well, then mulch the roots to conserve the water.

2 Water well as fruit starts to swell and during very dry spells of weather.

3 Feed every couple of weeks from spring onward, with an all-purpose liquid fertilizer.

4 Protect flowering plants with floating row cover against frost.

Problem solving

Poor air circulation causes powdery mildew (see p34), although resistant varieties such as 'Invicta' are available. Sawfly caterpillars can defoliate plants in no time so be vigilant from spring

Birds love gooseberries so cover plants tautly with netting.

Pick the first gooseberries when they are not fully ripe in late spring, leaving the rest to ripen fully for picking later on.

onward; remove any you see at once. Birds love not only the buds but also the sweet berries; net plants if birds are a nuisance.

Harvesting and storage

Gooseberries are best thinned in late spring when they are not quite ripe; harvest every other fruit and use them for jelly making. Pick the rest in summer. Wear gloves—the thorns are savage.

VARIETIES 'Greenfinch', 'Invicta', 'Leveller'

Expert tip

- To grow a cordon choose a strong branch to be the leader and clean off any shoots on its bottom 6in. (15cm). Then tie it to a cane. Cut back all other shoots to two buds. The following summer retie the leader and prune new growth to five leaves. That winter reduce the leader by one third and shorten all other shoots back to two buds. Do this every year.

Raspberries

Raspberries are delightfully easy and so low maintenance they can almost be ignored once planted. There are both summer- and fall-fruiting types. If you have room grow a pot of each for a long, delicious season.

Basic needs
Three plants should grow happily in a 12in. (30cm) pot. Add some grit to rich, soil-based potting mix for good drainage.

Growing techniques
1 Plant as bareroot or pot-grown plants, in midfall (see p59). Insert the plant so the soil mark on its canes is at ground level. This will encourage the production of lots of new canes.

2 Water, then place in a sunny, sheltered spot.

3 Mulch plants to conserve moisture.

4 Train canes up bamboo poles (see p59) or tie twine around them to stop them flopping.

5 Keep plants well fed and watered in summer.

Problem solving
Raspberries are affected by viruses and fungal diseases, which weaken plants and affect yields. Grow certified virus-free plants, keep on top of watering and feeding, and do not crowd plants. Good air circulation is vital. Dry patches on fruit with maggots inside are evidence of raspberry beetle. There is no cure; fall varieties are less susceptible. Birds can also be a

Fall-fruiting raspberry stems are cut down in late winter and reshoot in spring.

If raspberries are ripe they should separate cleanly from the plant. Pick when the weather is dry.

Expert tips

- Summer raspberries fruit on growth from the year before, so cut back old canes after harvesting (see p59).
- Fall varieties fruit on growth made in the current year. Wait until late winter to cut all the canes down. Thin out new canes in summer to stop overcrowding.
- Plants last about 10 years before becoming tired; then replace with new canes or root suckers of your own plants.

nuisance, although they do seem to find yellow-fruited varieties less palatable. Net the crops.

Harvesting and storage
Fruit should pull off the plant easily. Pick often to encourage further fruiting and prevent any missed fruit rotting and causing disease. Eat fresh or freeze, make into jelly, or bottle.

VARIETIES fall-fruiting: 'All Gold', 'Autumn Bliss'; summer-fruiting: 'Glen Ample', 'Glen Moy', 'Malling Jewel'

Raspberry perfection

Raspberries are a popular, homegrown crop and for very good reason—they are simple to grow, rewarding, and absolutely delicious. They grow well in pots and make handsome plants dripping with fruit.

When choosing your raspberry plants remember there are two types—summer and fall fruiting.

Only fall fruiters will give you a crop in their first year, since they fruit on the current year's growth. Their stems are all cut down in winter after they have finished fruiting, and new ones will sprout in spring to fruit again that fall. Summer-fruiting raspberries develop fruit on stems that grew the year before and so will not fruit until about 18 months after planting.

Plant bareroot raspberries in the dormant season and immediately cut summer-fruiting varieties down to 8in. (20cm) above the surface of the potting mix. When the new growth appears in spring tie it into supports. Canes fruit only once so cut them down after harvesting to make room for the new growth.

Once you have figured out this pruning routine, raspberries are fantastically easy to grow provided that you give them a sunny, sheltered spot and regular food, and mulch them to help the potting mix retain water.

In a pot either construct a framework of bamboo canes to support your raspberries or train plants against a wall.

Planting your raspberries

What you need

- 3 or 4 x raspberry canes, preferably bareroot;
- bucket of water;
- large pot, 12in. (30cm) or 16in. (40cm) in diameter;
- all-purpose potting mix;
- drainage material (see p15);
- pruners;
- bamboo canes and twine.

1 Unpack your bareroot canes as soon as they arrive and remove all their tags and packaging. Soak them in water for a couple of hours to rehydrate them and to reduce any further shock at planting. Fill the pot three quarters full of potting mix over some drainage material.

2 Plant quite shallowly, covering the roots with just 3½in. (8cm) of potting mix. Set three canes in a 12in. (30cm) pot, four in a 16in. (40cm) one. Water well and mulch. After planting summer-fruiting raspberries, shorten the canes back to 8in. (20cm) above the soil level. Water regularly during the growing season.

3 When the new shoots on summer raspberries appear in spring remove the old canes. Add a bamboo frame to the pot for support and tie in the young raspberry canes for cropping the following year.

4 Raspberry flowers are self fertile and will be visited by bees and other pollinating insects in spring, enabling plants to set fruit. Encourage healthy growth by feeding plants each year in spring.

5 Fruit is ripe when it separates from the plant leaving behind a clean plug. Keep picking to stimulate the development of more new fruit. When fruiting is over, cut down all these old fruiting canes.

Blueberries

Blueberries are deliciously sweet with a slight tang and so nutritious that they are celebrated as a "superfood." They are also attractive plants with vivid fall color and pretty bell flowers. Blueberries are perfect candidates for growing in containers, where you have total control over their conditions, because they are fussy, needing sun, and acidic, moist, well-drained soil. Give blueberries the right conditions and your plants will thrive.

Basic needs
Use acidic-soil mix to which some grit has been added to help drainage (see p63). Start young plants in pots 12in. (30cm) in diameter.

Growing techniques
1 Plant as bareroot or container plants in the fall or early spring. Then water each plant thoroughly.

2 Position the pot in a sheltered site where there is plenty of sun.

3 Keep the potting mix moist, but not waterlogged; nor should you let it dry out. If you can, water with rainwater rather than alkaline munipical water, which will gradually neutralize the potting mix and reduce your crop. If you have to use municipal water, topdress your pot with sulfur to maintain the acidic conditions.

4 Mulch plants with ericaceous materials such as bark, leafmold, or pine needles to lock in moisture around the roots.

5 Feed blueberry plants every month during the growing season with lime-free liquid fertilizer.

6 Blueberries are not totally hardy, hating the combination of cold and wet. In winter wrap pots with burlap or straw to protect plant roots against frost. In spring insulate flowers against late frosts by covering them with floating row cover.

7 Pot up every other year until you reach a final container size of 16–20in. (40–50cm) or more wide. After that, repot in fresh potting mix every 2–3 years.

Problem solving
Blueberries are comparatively trouble-free to grow, although birds are their biggest problem. Net plants if the birds get too greedy (see p63). Container plants are susceptible to powdery

Blueberries are such attractive plants they can hold their own beautifully with ornamental species such as this feather grass (*Stipa tenuissima*).

Blueberries are ripe when they are an even blue with a distinctive, white bloom.

mildew (see p34), which is a common problem when plants are too dry. Nip off any infected growth when you see it so it does not spread. You also need to improve your watering regime to prevent it from happening in the first place. Do this by mulching the plant and watering more regularly so the potting mix is always moist.

Harvesting and storage

Fruit is ready to pick when it is a deep, dark blue, from midsummer onwards. Pick over the plant several times as the fruit ripens gradually rather than all at the same time. Eat it fresh. You freeze or make blueberries into jellies or preserves.

VARIETIES early: 'Spartan'; midseason: 'Bluecrop' (self fertile), 'Chippewa' (self fertile), 'Northcountry' (self fertile), 'Northsky' (self fertile), 'Sunshine Blue' (self-fertile); late: 'Chandler' (self fertile), 'Duke'

Expert tips

- A few blueberry cultivars are self pollinating, but they are generally more productive when grown alongside two cross-pollinating partners. Three bushes should give you an ample crop.

- Do not worry about pruning in the first two years; just keep the plants open, and cut out dead, damaged, or diseased branches. After this prune in winter when plants are dormant. Remove a quarter of the dominant shoots and about half the weaker shoots to promote stronger growth.

- Place a saucer under each pot during the growing season to stop the potting mix drying out and losing nutrients. Remove it in winter so the plant does not become waterlogged.

Irresistible blueberries

Blueberries are picky plants demanding moist, light, acidic soil to thrive. They are therefore the perfect crop for a pot, where you can give them exactly what they need. They are also fine-looking plants with attractive flowers, fall leaf colors, and mouth-watering fruit, and they provide a great display in even the simplest terra-cotta pot.

If you're growing just one blueberry, make sure you plant a cultivar that will crop on its own, such as 'Sunshine Blue' or 'Bluecrop' (see p61). If you have the room though, it is well worth growing more than one to guarantee a big crop. Water the blueberry before planting in specialist acidic-soil mix. Never use ordinary all-purpose potting mix because it is too alkaline and would cause the plant to die slowly. Mulch with pine needles or bark, which will not upset the acidity of the soil. Give blueberries a sheltered, sunny spot.

Keep plants well watered with rainwater if you can, rather than using municipal water (see p60). During the growing season it can be helpful to place a saucer under the pot (see p61).

If you remove the fruit buds as they appear in the first year, you will get a much bigger harvest in the long run. In the second and subsequent years after planting feed blueberry plants with liquid 5–5–10 fertilizer once flowering begins.

Remember that berries ripen at different times, which means you need to keep checking and picking regularly so you don't miss any fruit.

Blueberries are a delicious fruit, often hailed as a superfood and expensive to buy in the stores, so they are well worth growing yourself.

Planting your blueberries

What you need

- terra-cotta pot 12in. (30cm) or more in diameter;
- drainage material (see p15);
- horticultural grit;
- acidic-soil mix;
- young blueberry plant;
- netting.

1 Line the bottom of the pot with drainage material to help water flow away freely. Mix horticultural grit into acidic-soil mix—you need about one part grit to two parts potting mix.

2 Water the blueberry well before planting it at the same level in the potting mix as it was in its previous pot. The crown of the plant should be just below the surface.

3 Water the plant well and keep the soil moist while the plant is establishing in the pot. Remember to use rainwater for watering because blueberries prefer it to municipal water. Then spread mulch around each plant. Water and feed plants regularly (see p60).

4 Protect your berries from greedy birds with netting, making sure it covers the plants completely but is held away from the fruit with canes so that the birds can't peck through it. Use the netting as soon as fruit buds appear since the birds relish these too.

5 Blueberries like warmth; give them as sunny a spot as you can so they can thrive and produce lots of their delicious berries. If the pot is in a hot, sunny spot, pay close attention to watering. Keep picking because the berries ripen at different times.

Currants

Currants are no trouble, look fantastic in full fruit, and have flowers rich in nectar. Red and white currants are quite sour and mainly used for cooking; they can be grown as cordons, fans, and standards. Black currants are vigorous plants, generally grown as bushes, and their fruit has a sweet tartness.

Basic needs

Black currants need a 16in. (40cm) pot; red and white currants can go in a 12in. (30cm) one. Use soil-based potting mix and grit (see p66).

Growing techniques

1 In the dormant season plant red and white currants at the same level as they were in the pot or ground. Black currants are planted slightly deeper (see p67). Water plants well.

2 Red and white currants tolerate more shade than black currants, although all fruit more quickly and sweetly when grown in the sun.

3 All currants benefit from mulch in spring and watering during dry spells. Feed with an all-purpose liquid fertilizer in the growing season.

4 Repot every two to three years into a pot of the same size or one only slightly larger. Use fresh potting mix and trim the roots back by one third.

Expert tips

- Prune in early spring. Black currants need one third of their oldest stems removing at the base. With other currants cut back to healthy buds, with the aim of maintaining 8–10 well-spaced branches.
- Lift containers up onto bricks in winter so that excess water can drain freely away.

Problem solving

Birds adore currants so protect your plants (see p67). Blister aphids can disfigure leaf undersides; look out for them in spring. Big bud mites can fatten black currant buds; dispose of infected buds and destroy heavily infested plants.

Harvesting and storage

Currants take longer to ripen than you think—they look ready before they are actually at their best. Cut as bunches and eat fresh, cooked, or make into jellies. They also freeze well.

VARIETIES black: 'Ben Connan', 'Ben Lomond', 'Ben Sarek'; red: 'Jonkheer van Tets', 'Red Lake', 'Stanza'; white: 'Versailles Blanche', 'White Grape'

White currants are slightly smaller and sweeter than red currants but can be used in the same way.

Leave red currants on the bush a little after they look ripe for them to sweeten further.

The longer black currants remain on the bush the sweeter they will be.

Grapes

Even in a small area, it is worth giving grape-growing a go. The vines are attractive in their own right, with their large, handsome leaves, and they can be encouraged to climb over a wall or fence, or grown as a standard if space is really tight. In a sunny site they will crop readily, and picking your own grapes, whether for eating or for making wine or juice, is a beautiful way to mark the end of the season.

Basic needs

Use soil-based potting mix combined with grit in a pot 12in. (30cm) or more wide (see p69).

Growing techniques

1 Plant from late fall to late spring (see p68). Water and mulch. Place in a very sunny spot.

2 Once tiny fruit appear give plants a weekly liquid 5–5–10 feed.

3 Water well during dry spells, particularly in the first year after planting.

4 Remove all flowers in the first two years; allow only three bunches of grapes on three-year-old plants; then five on four-year-old plants. After this they can flower and fruit freely.

5 Refresh the top 6in. (15cm) of potting mix every spring.

Problem solving

Protect fruit against wasps and birds with netting or wrap individual bunches with cheesecloth or old panty hose. Fungal growth on leaves may be a sign of powdery or downy mildew. The former can spread to stems and fruit (see p34). Gray mold may infect developing bunches of fruit. Ensure that vines are adequately watered to prevent the problem and prune overcrowded shoots.

Harvesting and storage

Grapes are ready when they feel soft, but taste is the better indicator of when to pick. Sometime

Expert tips

- Prune in early winter by cutting all growth back to one or two buds for tight, compact growth.
- Train and thin out young shoots in spring and summer.
- Nip off the leaves around fruit so that the sun can reach the grapes, for ripening.

between late summer and midfall the fruit should turn sweet and sugary, when the bunches can be cut. Eat dessert grapes right away or store in the refrigerator for a couple of weeks. Wine grapes can be eaten but are best made into juice or wine.

VARIETIES red wine: 'New York Muscat'; white wine: 'Chardonnay', 'Seyval Blanc'; red dessert: 'Schiava Grossa'; white dessert: 'Muscat of Alexandria', 'Siegerrebe'; dual-purpose: 'Boskoop Glory'

Expose young fruit to sunlight by picking off any leaves that may delay ripening.

Black currant "superfruits"

These old favorites are bursting with Vitamin C and are expensive in the stores, so are a double delight to grow yourself. They are easy-care, highly productive plants—provided you get to the fruit before the birds! A decorative, glazed container will complement the plant nicely, and it's less porous than terra-cotta, so will hold water for longer. Once the fruit have been harvested, pick the leaves to make a lovely tea.

Plant bareroot plants between midfall and winter in a sunny site. Black currants are vigorous growers needing a larger pot than other currants (see p64) and are usually grown as a bush rather than trained in any other way. Plant in a 2:1 mix of soil-based potting mix and horticultural grit, to aid drainage. Black currants are planted so that part of the stem is buried, in order to encourage lots of young, vigorous shoots to develop from the base. This will give you a productive, multistemmed bush. Directly after planting cut down some of the shoots; although it will lead to a smaller crop in the first year, the result will be a stronger plant. If planting a container-grown black currant at any other time of year wait until midfall to early spring to do this pruning.

Black currants are particularly hungry and thirsty plants so give them a good mulch in spring and feed and water them well in the growing season.

Bushes do not need pruning the year after planting. Thereafter in early spring cut down up to one third of the old stems almost to soil level—these are a darker color. This will encourage an open habit and young, fresh growth from the base, which will produce fruit later that season. Repot every two to three years (see opposite).

The leaves of black currants have a distinctive sweet, currantlike scent when crushed, which is a good way to tell one currant from another when they are not in fruit.

Planting a bareroot black currant

What you need

- bareroot black currant plant (see p64);
- bucket of water;
- drainage material (see p15);
- large, ornamental pot 16in. (40cm) or more in diameter;
- soil-based potting mix;
- all-purpose, slow-release fertilizer (see p15);
- pruners;
- netting.

1 Soak the bareroot plant in a bucket of water as soon as you get it home. Add a layer of drainage material to the base of the pot and then half fill it with potting mix. Add some fertilizer to help the roots establish quickly and get your plant off to the best start.

2 Plant your black currant deeply, so that the crown is about 3½in. (8cm) below the surface of the potting mix. This will promote fresh, strong growth from the base. Work the potting mix around the roots and then fill the rest of the pot with the mix, firming it well. Water thoroughly and top up the potting mix if necessary.

3 After planting cut back some of the stems to 1¼in. (3cm) high, using pruners. Then add a layer of mulch. Water and feed plants regularly.

4 Protect developing fruit from birds by netting plants in early summer. Stretch the netting tautly so the birds cannot peck through it or get caught in it.

5 Harvest modern varieties of black currant by snipping off entire strings. Older types ripen gradually, so fruit should be picked individually.

Grapes on the vine

If you choose your grape variety carefully (see p65) and provide a warm, sunny spot, you should be rewarded with grapes for juicing, wine, or simply eating straight off the vine. In containers, grow the grape as a standard, especially if space is limited. Why not invest in a plant already trained to save you time and bring you closer to your first harvest?

Grapes do well in pots, and in a large one 16in. (40cm) wide and deep you could be cropping from the same plant for years. It is advisable however to remove all flowers for the first couple of years (see p65). With the right pruning a grape vine makes an attractive plant—many have magnificent fall color too. Ideally container-grown plants should be planted in late spring when growth has already started, while bareroot vines can be planted any time between late fall and early spring. Grapes like free-draining potting mix, but one that doesn't dry out too quickly, so choose a soil-based one and add some grit. These plants need as much sunshine as you can give them to produce the sugars that make the fruit deliciously sweet, so save your warmest, sunniest spot for them. In front of a sunny wall is perfect. The ideal conditions for a grape however are cool roots, so mulch with large pebbles or include a low-growing plant, such as cranesbill (*Geranium*), to help shield the pot from direct sunlight. Also group the pot with others so they provide shade.

Above: To deflect the sun off the grape's roots include a low-growing plant such as this cranesbill in the pot; it will act as a living mulch and help to keep the pot cool.

Left: Keep on top of watering and feeding and your pot-grown grape should happily produce an abundance of healthy, juicy bunches.

Planting your grape

What you need

■ terra-cotta pot 16in. (40cm) or more wide and deep;
■ drainage material (see p15); ■ soil-based potting mix; ■ horticultural grit;
■ slow-release fertilizer (see p15); ■ standard grape vine;
■ netting.

1 Line the base of the pot with drainage material. Then half fill the pot with the potting mix.

2 Work in a handful of the fertilizer with a trowel. Place the vine, while still in its original pot, on the potting mix to ensure the plant will be at the same depth as it was previously planted. Adjust the potting mix depth as appropriate.

3 Remove the vine's pot and place the plant in the center of the new pot. Fill around the rootball with potting mix and firm evenly. Then insert the low-growing plant. Water everything in well and mulch.

4 Water your plant regularly in dry summers (see p65). Start feeding your plants once the small bunches of fruit appear, giving them liquid 5–5–10 feed each week.

5 Taking care not to nip the developing fruit, remove the leaves around the bunches so the sun can reach them. Protect ripening fruit from the birds with netting. Pick when fruit is sweet and sugary (see p65).

Strawberries

The compact, trailing habit of strawberries makes them ideal for pots or baskets. Also, since the fruits are off the ground, they are easier to look after and to pick, and they are also less vulnerable to slugs and snails. If you grow a combination of different varieties, it is possible to have sweet, fresh strawberries from late spring right through to the fall. Each variety of June-bearing strawberry has a short but heavy cropping period of two or three weeks, and there are early, mid-, and late fruiting varieties cropping from early to midsummer. Everbearering strawberries, also known as perpetuals, are different: they produce small flushes of fruit continuously from early summer to early fall.

Basic needs

Use any pot, hanging basket (see pp72–3), window box, or even grow bag that is 4in. (10cm) or more deep. Six plants will grow well in a basket 14in. (35cm) wide; four or five in a grow bag, window box, or pot 8in. (20cm) wide. Don't be tempted to grow too many in one pot. Fill each container with good-quality, all-purpose potting mix.

Growing techniques

1 In late summer or early fall plant strawberries so they have time to get their roots settled before the cold weather sets in. You can also plant in early spring but

Take care to plant young runners at the correct depth, with the crown level with the soil.

you will not get a big crop that first year. Make sure the crown is level with the soil surface. If strawberries are planted too deeply they rot; if too high they dry out and die. After planting water well.

2 Give plants a sheltered, sunny spot.

3 Water well and apply an all-purpose liquid fertilizer after planting to help plants establish. Strawberries are shallow-rooting and dry out quickly, so water little and often to keep the soil moist but without waterlogging it.

Expert tips

- Grow only certified, virus-free varieties purchased from reliable suppliers.
- Covering plants with temporary row cover in early spring will encourage flowering, and so fruiting, a week earlier than normal. Remove the cover during the day to help visiting insects pollinate flowers.
- If growing on a windy site or you simply want to ensure a decent crop, pollinate flowers yourself with a small brush.
- Cut off runners, unless you want to propagate new plants, to keep energy focused on flower and fruit production.
- After cropping remove all the old leaves, stems, and runners, as well as straw. Then feed plants with all-purpose liquid fertilizer.
- Replace plants after three or four years, when their cropping potential declines.
- Strawberries are easy plants to propagate—allow runners to root and then transplant into individual pots.
- Alpine strawberries, which are smaller than other types, also do brilliantly in pots. They produce tiny strawberries from early summer right up to the frosts.

A terra-cotta, purposemade strawberry jar is a handy and fun way to grow a crop of strawberries in a small space.

Harvest strawberries as soon as they are ripe, preferably on a hot, sunny day when the warmth will enhance their flavor.

4 Mulch with straw to conserve water and keep fruit clean and dry.

5 Regular feeding is essential for container-grown strawberries, so give liquid 5–5–10 fertilizer every week or so when these plants are flowering and fruiting.

Problem solving

In damp conditions gray mold can be a big problem so always water from below and ensure good air circulation around plants. Birds can be a nuisance too; drape pots with netting. Protect plants against slugs and snails (see p32).

Harvesting and storage

Strawberries are ready for picking when they are a luscious, bright red all over. Harvest them at the warmest time of day for sweet, fragrant fruit. Pick just before eating as strawberries do not keep well. Some varieties such as 'Totem' freeze well, and all can be made into jellies.

VARIETIES early: 'Hapil', 'Honeoye', 'Korona'; mid: 'Alice', 'Cambridge Favourite', 'Pegasus', 'Totem'; late: 'Florence', 'Rhapsody', 'Symphony'; everbearing: 'Aromel', Mara des Bois', 'Viva Rosa'

Growing strawberries in holes cut into grow bags saves you having to worry about mulching with straw or plastic.

Strawberry basket

There is something very special about these delicious and gloriously perfumed fruit, and by having your own crop you can pick strawberries when they are at their absolute peak. Fruit grown in a hanging basket will be well away from pesky slugs, and a basket is also a small area to net against birds, which can peck at the crop. As you can grow only a few plants at the top of each basket, give it an added dash by lining it with a pretty oil cloth.

Grow six plants in a 14in. (35cm) hanging basket. Although you can use fewer plants in a smaller container (see p70), don't be tempted to have too many plants because overcrowding can cause fungal disease. Buy strawberries as young, potted plants or bareroot runners and plant in late summer to early fall or in spring. To encourage roots to establish and to get a bigger harvest the following year, pinch back the flowers of spring-planted strawberries in the first year.

Keep strawberries well watered—this probably means watering most days during the growing season (see p70). Fill the pot in the center of the basket (see step 3, right), rather than watering the soil directly. As soon as flowers appear, feed with liquid 5–5–10 fertilizer every 7–10 days. At the end of the season give plants a tidy-up, clearing away old leaves, stems, and fruit as well as the straw mulch. This will help expose the crowns to the cold over the winter, which will induce the necessary dormant period for the production of new crowns the following year.

Above: Bees love strawberry flowers and they will buzz around them, pollinating as they go. They dislike windy spots so make sure your basket is sheltered.

Left: For the sweetest, most fragrant fruit, pick during the warmest time of day. Hold the stem and break or cut it off; do not pull the strawberries since they bruise very readily.

Planting your hanging basket

What you need
- hanging basket and liner;
- piece of oil cloth large enough to line the basket;
- marker pen and scissors;
- all-purpose soilless mix;
- 6 x strawberry plants;
- small plastic pot;
- straw or fiber mat.

1 Using the basket liner as a template, draw the liner shape onto the oil cloth with the pen. Then cut out the circular shape marked on the oil cloth.

2 Place the oil cloth in the basket, making sure it is evenly spaced all around the edge. Then puncture some holes in the oil cloth with scissors. Add the liner and fill the basket two thirds full with all-purpose soilless mix.

3 Sink a small pot with drainage holes in the center of the basket—this will help you to water evenly. Then space the strawberry plants evenly around the edge of the basket. Before you water well, add more soilless mix to fill in. Water and feed plants regularly.

4 Once fruit appears, mulch with straw or a fiber mat to keep the strawberries away from damp soil. This will stop them rotting and help to conserve moisture. Strawberries hate their roots sitting in damp soil so water them little and often.

5 Pick fruit as soon as it is ripe—strawberries should be a deep, even red all over. Check plants regularly so you don't miss any. Overripe fruit will soon start to break down and rot so it must be discarded immediately, before it becomes diseased.

Vegetables

Tomatoes

All tomatoes are ideal for growing in containers. There are three types: indeterminate, which need staking and pinching back as they grow (see p80); determinate types, which require less maintenance; and semideterminate ones, which are excellent in hanging baskets (see p78). You can buy young plants in spring, but if you use seed you'll have a wider choice.

Basic needs

Grow in containers 12–18in. (30–45cm) deep filled with soil-based potting mix, or try using grow bags.

When potting up ensure the tomato stem is buried right up to its first leaves, to encourage further roots from the stem.

You can help flowers set and turn to fruit either by misting them with water or by tapping the flowers.

Growing techniques

1 In early spring place four or five seeds on top of the moist seed starter mix in a small pot. Cover it with plastic wrap to keep humidity levels high.

2 Place the pot on a warm, sunny windowsill. Seeds should germinate within two weeks.

3 Prick on the seedlings into individual pots.

4 Pot them up into larger pots a few weeks later. Once the weather is warm enough and they are big enough to go outside into their final pots, plant one tomato per pot (two per grow bag) right up to its first leaves. This will help anchor the plant in the pot.

5 In early summer gradually harden the plants, acclimatizing them to the outdoors over a couple of weeks, before leaving them in direct sun or bright, filtered light outdoors by midsummer.

6 Stake indeterminate tomatoes as they grow, using canes and twine. You should have only one main stem so pinch back any sideshoots that form in the leaf joints (see p81). Once five trusses

Expert tips

- Water plants so that the soil is always moist but do not overdo it. Too much water can lead to disease and can cause nutrients to leach out of the soil as well as reduced flavor in fruit.

- Tomatoes are ripe when they are all one color. Any stragglers still on the plant at the end of summer will not redden before the frosts so bring them indoors to ripen.

- Help your tomatoes by growing companions plants nearby: It is said marigolds keep away whitefly and encourage bees for pollination; borage deters tomato hornworm; and basil makes the flavor of your tomatoes even better.

Carrots and tomatoes are believed to be beneficial companion plants when grown together.

Tomatoes retain their good qualities if left on the plant when ripe but will lose their flavor if stored in the refrigerator.

have developed pinch back the top of the plant two leaves above the last truss. This will ensure all your tomatoes have time to ripen before the frosts. Determinate and semideterminate tomatoes are left to grow naturally; they do not need any staking, support, or pinching back.

7 Water plants regularly and feed once a week with liquid 5–5–10 fertilizer after the first flowers have developed.

Problem solving

Most problems can be kept at bay with consistent watering and feeding. Irregular watering will cause fruit to split, although these are still perfectly edible. Erratic watering combined with a lack of calcium in the soil can lead to blossom end rot, which makes the bottom of tomatoes turn a leathery black. In wet summers look out

for tomato late blight—chocolate-brown patches on leaves and blackening stems (see p35). Be vigilant and act quickly if these symptoms appear. At the first signs of tomato late blight it is best to pick all your fruit, letting it ripen indoors.

Harvesting and storage

Ripe tomatoes will happily remain on the plant for a couple of weeks, which is handy as they taste best when eaten fresh. They will keep at room temperature for four or five days and can be frozen as purée or ready-made sauces. Tomatoes can also be bottled or dried as well as made into pickles and chutneys.

VARIETIES determinate: 'Legend', Tornado'; indeterminate: 'Gardener's Delight', 'Sungold'; semideterminate: 'Hundreds and Thousands'

Cherry tomato basket

If you are running out of room, hanging baskets are the answer. They make the most of your vertical space, look fantastic, and can be really productive. Determinate and semideterminate tomatoes have been specially bred to grow in small pots and baskets, and with their spreading habit will spill over and down the sides. They produce masses of sweet, aromatic fruit too, and are brilliantly low maintenance.

For your hanging basket choose a coconut or sisal liner rather than the more traditional sphagnum moss one, and add a circle of plastic, cut from an old soil-mix bag, to the base to aid water retention. Tomatoes are hungry and thirsty plants so one will be enough for a standard basket, 14in. (35cm) wide. When planting, sit the basket in a large plant pot to keep it stable if it is wobbling. All-purpose soilless mix is best in baskets as soil-based ones are too heavy when wet. To help retain moisture during a dry summer or the times when you cannot be around to water, mix water-retaining crystals into the soilless mix before you plant. Keep the mix moist (see p76), which may well mean watering every day, and as soon as flowers appear start feeding your tomato plants weekly.

Opposite: A tomato in a hanging basket can be just as eye-catching as one filled with summer flowers. If possible hang it by the kitchen door for easy pickings.

Planting your tomato basket

What you need
■ hanging basket; ■ coconut or sisal liner; ■ circle of plastic, cut from an old soil-mix bag; ■ all-purpose soilless mix; ■ water-retaining crystals; ■ slow-release fertilizer (optional); ■ semideterminate type tomato (see p77).

1 Place the liner in the hanging basket, keeping it flush at the edges. Line the bottom with some plastic from an old soil-mix bag. Fill about two thirds of the basket with soilless mix.

2 Add some water-retaining crystals, according to the manufacturer's instructions, and fork it into the soilless mix well. You can also add some slow-release fertilizer (see p15) at this stage if you wish.

3 Plant the tomato in the center of the basket, as deep as its first true leaves, and fill in with soilless mix, firming as you go. Leave a gap between the mix and the top of the basket to make watering easier. Water well after planting.

4 As soon as the first yellow flowers begin to form, give your plant liquid 5–5–10 fertilizer every week. (Our plant was already in flower so we fed it straight after planting.) Keep the soil moist by watering these thirsty plants very regularly.

5 Tomatoes are always at their most delicious when eaten fresh and warmed by the sunshine. Try to pick them straight from the vine whenever possible.

Long Tom tomato

The taste of a homegrown tomato fresh from the vine is unbeatable—a rich, sweet tang that's missing from even the best store-bought fruit, and for this reason alone they are one of the most popular crops to grow. Give them a helping hand and ensure the best harvest possible by growing them with companions such as French marigolds (*Tagetes patula*) and basil. Some people believe basil deters whitefly and even intensifies the flavor of the fruit, while marigolds will encourage pollinating bees.

There are hundreds of different varieties of tomato available, from the tender cherry to burly beefsteaks (see p77), and all of them can be started from seed indoors in early spring, by sowing them in small pots and placing them on a warm, sunny windowsill (see p76). They will need potting up into larger pots after about seven weeks and can be planted outside in early summer. Alternatively you can buy young plants from the garden center or by mail order. Harden young plants for a few days before planting out and then give them the warmest, sunniest spot in your yard. Grow only one plant per container as tomatoes are hungry, thirsty plants. Their soil mustn't dry out, which will mean watering every day in hot weather.

Make sure you know which tomato type you are growing, as indeterminate tomatoes need to be tied into stakes, and their sideshoots pinched back. Give plants a weekly liquid 5–5–10 feed once the flowers appear. Pick the marigold flowers.

Above: Harvest the tomatoes when they are a gorgeous red all over and eat them right away. They will ripen gradually up the vine as you continue cropping.

Left: Keeping on top of regular tasks such as pinching back sideshoots and tying the tomato to its cane will result in a tall, slender plant on a single stem.

Planting your long Tom tomato

What you need
- small pots, all-purpose soilless mix, indeterminate tomato seed, and plastic wrap, if sowing; ■ tall, terra-cotta pot; ■ drainage material (see p15); ■ soil-based potting mix; ■ bamboo cane and twine; ■ 3 x basil, 3 x marigold.

1 Sow four or five seeds in a small pot of moist all-purpose soilless mix in early spring, cover with plastic wrap, and place on a sunny windowsill. Keep the potting mix moist. Pot up plants into individual pots (see p76). Grow on until it is warm enough for the plants to go outside.

2 In early summer line the base of the final pot with drainage material. Then half fill it with soil-based potting mix. Plant one tomato deeply in the center of the pot, burying it up to its first set of healthy leaves (see p76). Top up the potting mix and water the plant well.

3 Stake the tomato plant, tying it to the cane with twine. Then insert the basil and marigold plants around the tomato, and water the plants again and mulch. (If you prefer, you could plant up your other seed-raised tomato plants similarly.)

4 Keep tying the tomato into the cane as it develops. Feed and water plants regularly. Nip off the growing points of the basil to make stockier plants and discourage flowering. Harvest the basil leaves regularly.

5 Pinch back any sideshoot that grows in a leaf joint between the main stem and a side branch. Once the tomato has grown five trusses, pinch back the top of the plant two leaves above the last truss. Pick the tomatoes as they mature.

Eggplants

With their exotic, purple flowers, plump, glossy fruit, and beautiful, downy leaves, eggplants make a handsome sight. An array of colors and sizes is available, but the fruit all have the same delicious, creamy taste.

Basic needs
Grow in a pot 12in. (30cm) in diameter filled with good-quality, all-purpose potting mix, for a single plant. Dwarf varieties will fit into something a little smaller. Three plants will grow happily in a grow bag.

Growing techniques
1 Eggplants require long, hot summers, so if growing in cool-temperate areas choose varieties with small, slender fruit, which need less ripening (see p84). Grow them from young plants to give them sufficient time to develop and ripen; grafted plants may give you even more of a headstart.

2 If growing from seed, sow in early spring and place the pot on a warm, light windowsill, at 68°F (20°C). Do not let the soil dry out.

3 When big enough to handle, prick seedlings on into individual pots. They can be planted out into their final pots when frosts have definitely passed,

Ripe, glossy eggplants such as this one are delicious when sliced and roasted in olive oil over a barbecue in summer.

but harden them for a few days first.

4 Grow eggplants in your hottest, sunniest spot, preferably against a warm wall.

5 Once the first fruit appears, feed every two weeks with liquid 5–5–10 fertilizer.

Expert tips

- Once plants reach 12in. (30cm) pinch back the main tip to encourage sideshoots.
- Stake larger plants.
- Help fruiting by tapping flowers to release pollen, rubbing them with a small paint brush, or misting with water.
- Remove petals sticking to fruit to prevent gray mold.
- Nip off lower leaves as the fruit swells to improve air flow.

Problem solving
Mist foliage daily to deter red spider mite. Rub aphids off by hand whenever they are seen (see p34). Remove growth infected by gray mold at once. Regular watering prevents blossom end rot.

Harvesting and storage
Pick fruit when fully colored and glossy. It will keep for a couple of weeks in the refrigerator. Eggplant can be pickled or frozen in sauces.

VARIETIES 'Amethyst', 'Baby Belle', 'Baby Rosanna', 'Calliope', 'Fairy Tale', 'Falcon', 'Galine', 'Mohican', 'Moneymaker', 'Slim Jim'

Sweet & chili peppers

Both sweet and chili peppers are definitely worth growing, but they do need a long, sunny season. There's a world of difference between store-bought and homegrown peppers so give different shapes and colors a try. Why not give yourself a headstart by growing on young plants, especially grafted ones—it will make a successful harvest much more likely.

Basic needs

Grow in a container 12in. (30cm) in diameter with good drainage and filled with all-purpose potting mix, one for each plant. Three plants will fit in a grow bag. Very compact varieties will also grow in a hanging basket.

Growing techniques

1 Grow from young plants (see p86), or sow indoors from late winter to midspring (see p87).

2 Keep well watered and be patient—seeds can be slow to germinate.

3 Place the pot in a hot, sunny spot—the base of a warm wall is ideal (see p86) or grow peppers under glass.

4 Water regularly in dry weather, and when flowering apply an all-purpose liquid fertilizer.

Problem solving

Usually trouble-free.

Harvesting and storage

Although sweet and chili peppers come in a range of colors, they generally mature from green through to red. Pick fruit at whichever stage of color you prefer (see p87). Eat fresh, slow-dry them in the oven, or hang up to air dry (see p86).

VARIETIES chili peppers: 'Apache', 'Chenzo', 'Fiesta', 'Filius Blue', 'Gusto Purple', 'Hungarian Hot Wax'; sweet peppers: 'Ace', 'Gourmet', 'Marconi Rosso', 'Mohawk', 'Redskin', 'Roberta'

Pinch back the growing tips of plants when they have reached 8in. (20cm), or just above the fifth set of leaves. This will encourage bushy growth (see above) and lots more fruit.

Some chili peppers should be harvested when they are still green to encourage the plant to fruit further. The other fruits can then be left to redden at the end of the season.

Expert tips

- Pinch back growing tips to encourage bushy growth.
- Assist pollination by brushing flower to flower with a paint brush.
- Get a headstart by overwintering plants in a warm glasshouse or sunroom. Prune them well and water sparingly.

Shiny, black eggplants

Eggplants are an expensive vegetable in the stores and don't taste a patch on the flavorsome smoothness of ones you can grow yourself. Large pots, which are needed for a good crop, can be expensive, so adapt other containers such as black, plastic storage crates for a good, cheap alternative. They also set off the polished, black fruit beautifully.

Eggplants need a really long, hot growing season, so, if there is one crop you are going to grow from a young plant bought at the garden center rather than grow it from seed, this is it. Don't worry about cheating—you need all the help you can get with eggplants, especially if you are growing them in a cool-temperate area. Get plants as soon as they appear on the shelves and pot them on, growing them on a bright, warm windowsill until the weather is warm enough for them to go in their crates outside.

Give eggplants your brightest, hottest spot. Once they reach 8–12in. (20–30cm), pinch back the growing tips (see opposite) to promote bushy growth. As soon as flowering begins, give plants a weekly feed with liquid 5–5–10 fertilizer and brush the flowers to assist pollination (see p82). Larger fruiting varieties may need staking with a cane to keep them upright.

Opposite: Harvest fruit when it is still a shiny, glossy indigo-black or it will quickly turn bitter.

Planting your eggplant crate

What you need
- black plastic storage crate;
- screwdriver or drill;
- drainage material (see p15);
- all-purpose potting mix;
- 2 x eggplant plants (see p82).

1 Any container that is not specifically a plant pot will always need holes punched or drilled into the base if it does not already have them. Then add a layer of drainage material and fill two thirds of the crate with potting mix.

2 Position plants on the potting mix surface while still in their pots to establish the correct planting depth—this should be the same as it is in each pot. Then remove each plant from its pot and plant, adding more potting mix to fill. Water in well, then mulch.

3 Eggplants are large, hungry, thirsty plants and particularly when grown in pots, so water regularly, never letting them dry out and protect them from slugs and snails (see p32). Give them a liquid 5–5–10 feed once a week.

4 When each plant reaches 8–12in. (20–30cm) high nip off its growing tip with your fingertips to encourage fresh, bushy growth and quicker, heavier, earlier fruiting.

5 Fruit is best picked when young and shiny, otherwise it has a tendency to turn woolly inside and develop masses of bitter-tasting seeds. Early cropping also encourages further ripening.

Chili pepper hot pots

The spicy kick of a chili pepper can transform so many dishes, and it packs quite a punch in the yard too. It is well worth giving it a decent pot, such as these classic terra-cotta planters, rather than settling for plastic ones. Growers get quite fanatical about chili peppers, and there are now hundreds of varieties to choose from, so take your pick. Grow a collection and you will have enough to see you well into the new year.

Chili peppers can be sown any time from late winter until the end of spring, but the earlier you sow the longer the plants have to ripen. Late winter is the ideal time. Alternatively you can buy young plants, which are readily available from garden centers and by mail order (see p83). However such sources do not offer the same variety of color and shape that you get from seed nurseries. Cover freshly sown seed with plastic wrap to keep humidity levels up and promote germination, and keep the potting mix moist. When planting outside give plants a sheltered, sunny spot—the hotter the better—because they need a long, warm summer to ripen. Pinching back the growing tips will promote bushier growth and therefore more fruit (see p83). Large, heavily laden plants may well need help by tying them onto two or more supporting canes. Feed with liquid 5–5–10 fertilizer once a week when the flowers appear, and give the bees a hand by pollinating flowers yourself with a small brush or cotton-tipped probe. Leaving the first set of fruit on the plant to mature to red will result in far fewer peppers, so harvest the first fruit when they are green and then you'll get fruit right through into the fall.

Above: An attractive way of drying chili peppers is to thread string or cotton through each fruit and hang in the warm.

Left: The hotter the chili, such as the habaneros (in the right-hand pot), the longer it can take to ripen, which is well worth keeping in mind in cool-temperate areas.

Sowing your chili seeds

What you need

- small pots for sowing and growing on; ▪ all-purpose soilless mix; ▪ chili pepper seeds—3 different varieties (see p83); ▪ plastic wrap; ▪ terra-cotta pots at least 12in. (30cm) wide; ▪ canes and twine; ▪ drainage material (see p15).

1 Fill 2½in. (7cm) pots with the potting mix, firming it down gently to remove any air holes. Water the potting mix to moisten it before sowing. Sow two seeds per pot. Cover the seed by sprinkling lightly with more potting mix, then water again gently.

2 Cover the pots with plastic wrap. Place on a warm, light windowsill. Remove the plastic wrap after germination. When seedlings sprout a second set of leaves, nip off the weaker seedling to leave one healthy plant in each pot. Keep the soil moist.

3 When the young plants reach about 5in. (12cm) high, pot them on into larger pots. Water well. Once they reach 8in. (20cm) high, tie each plant to a small bamboo cane for support. Protect plants from attack by slugs and snails (see p32).

4 As soon as all frosts have passed, the plants can go out into their final pots. Cover each base with a good layer of drainage material, then fill with potting mix and plant up. Stake each plant. Initially cover with a temporary row cover in cool-temperate areas.

5 Water and feed plants regularly. Rather than leave the first fruit to turn red, snip off the first chili peppers when they are still green. You will then get more fruit, and these can be left on the plant to ripen fully to a bright, glossy red.

Zucchini

Zucchini are one of the quickest, easiest, and most productive crops, and are definitely worth growing considering how much they cost in the stores. But do not overdo it—you only need one or two plants to keep you in an abundance of zucchini all summer long. Despite taking up lots of room in the veg garden, they are very happy in large pots, especially if you choose a compact variety.

Basic needs

Zucchini are hungry, thirsty plants so use a large container, 2ft. (60cm) wide, or a grow bag. Mix potting mix with well-rotted manure and a sprinkle of all-purpose fertilizer.

Growing techniques

1 Sow seed in late spring, or grow from store-bought plants in early summer. Set 2–3 seeds on their sides in the pot or grow bag and place in a warm, sunny spot.

2 Thin to leave one strong seedling per pot.

3 Keep potting mix moist, particularly once the fruit starts to swell. Water around plants rather than over them, to prevent rotting.

4 Once fruit appears feed every couple of weeks with 5–5–10 or all-purpose liquid fertilizer.

Problem solving

Protect pots against slugs (see p32). Prevent

powdery mildew by keeping plants well watered, particularly during late summer (see p34).

Try harvesting with flowers still attached. These can be fried whole or tossed into salads.

By picking zucchini when they are still young you will promote a large, continuous harvest.

Expert tips

- Since zucchini seeds are large, flat, and have a tendency to rot, always sow them on their narrow sides.

- Sinking a small plant pot into the potting mix next to the plant and watering into it will ensure the water goes down to the plant's roots where it is needed, and doesn't sit around the crown causing rot.

Harvesting and storage

Harvest from midsummer to midfall when zucchini are about 4in. (10cm) long. Keep picking regularly so they do not get too big. Eat fresh; chop, blanch, and freeze; or make into jellies or pIckles. Flowers are also lovely in salads or when stuffed and fried.

VARIETIES bush: 'Bambino', 'Jemmer', 'Romanesco', 'Tristan', 'Venus'; climbing: 'Black Forest', 'Tondo Chairo di Nizza', 'Tromboncino'

Cucumbers

Cucumbers are gratifyingly easy to grow, asking only for sun and something to climb up before rewarding you with heaps of fruit and beautiful, bright flowers. The longer, smooth-skinned, slicing varieties need a warm, humid environment, while smaller, prickly outdoor cucumbers grow very happily in cool-temperate climates—just choose a variety to suit your conditions.

Basic needs
Grow individually in any pot, tub, trough, or grow bag provided it is 10in. (25cm) in diameter and 8in. (20cm) deep. Fill the container with soil-based potting mix.

Growing techniques
1 In midspring sow seed in warm conditions, a minimum temperature of 68°F (20°C), or buy young plants in late spring. Sow the seeds on their sides to prevent rotting, and cover (see p91).

2 Grow in a warm, sheltered site or under glass, and mulch plants to conserve moisture.

3 Keep the potting mix moist, watering around

Cucumbers are attractive, exotic-looking plants with their large, tropical leaves, golden flowers, and prolific fruit.

plants rather than over them (see p90).

4 Train longer, smooth-skinned, slicing varieties up a tepee, canes, or trellis. Smaller types can be left to trail over the pot.

5 Feed every two weeks with a liquid 5–5–10 fertilizer once the fruit starts to develop.

Problem solving
Protect pots against slugs (see p32). Ensure plants are always moist to prevent powdery mildew (see p34); remove affected leaves at once and spray with water to keep conditions humid.

Harvesting and storage
The skin toughens with age so pick cucumbers young. Store in the refrigerator for up to a week.

VARIETIES indoors: 'Bella', 'Femdan', 'Zeina'; outdoors: 'Chinese Slangen', 'Crystal Lemon', 'Marketmore', 'Tokyo Slicer'

Expert tips

- Choose F_1 cultivars of smooth-skinned, slicing types, as they are all-female plants. Otherwise plants will need their male flowers removed to stop them pollinating the female ones and causing bitter fruit.

- Plants hate root disturbance so either sow cucumbers in their final pots or in biodegradable pots to reduce stress later.

- Place a collar around each plant stem to stop it rotting (see p91).

- Focus energy into fruit production by pinching back the growing tips.

Climbing cucumber

A single cucumber in a large pot will keep you in crisp, juicy fruit all summer long. In fact you may have trouble keeping up with these prolific plants. Despite their striking, exotic looks they are surprisingly easy to grow—just give them a warm spot, plenty of food and water, and keep on picking!

Make sure you have chosen the right cucumber to grow outdoors, as indoor types will not cope in the cooler conditions outdoors (see p89). Cucumbers hate having their roots disturbed; therefore, if growing from seed, sow into biodegradable pots and you can plant them out, pot and all. Harden plants gradually over a week or so, before planting them outside in a warm, sunny, sheltered place. Alternatively sow seed directly outside at the beginning of summer and cover with temporary row cover such as a large glass jar, or grow them under glass.

Pinch back the growing tip once seven leaves have developed, and then train the sideshoots up and around an obelisk, pinching out flowerless shoots after five leaves. Growing cucumbers up such a support saves space. You can however also let cucumbers trail over the side of the pot and along the ground. Being almost all water, cucumbers are very thirsty plants, particularly in pots, so keep them well watered. Unfortunately they are very susceptible to rot, so water around the plant rather than drenching the leaves and stems. Every two weeks give them liquid 5–5–10 fertilizer once the fruit starts to appear.

A cucumber plant dripping with fruit can be heavy, so ensure that it is securely tied to its support and that the support is well embedded in the container.

Sowing your cucumber seed

What you need
- small biodegradable pots;
- all-purpose potting mix;
- cucumber seeds (see p89);
- plastic wrap; ■ pot at least 12in. (30cm) wide and deep;
- drainage material (see p15);
- collar made from old plastic pot; ■ obelisk; ■ twine.

1 Sow two seeds on their sides in each biodegradable pot filled with potting mix. Cover with plastic wrap and place on a warm, bright windowsill. Remove the plastic wrap after germination. Snip off the weakest seedling. As the plant grows, pot it up.

2 When ready, plant the cucumber just off-center in the final pot, filled with potting mix and a layer of drainage. Make sure the top of the rootball is level with the soil surface. To stop the stem rotting make a collar by cutting away the base of an old plastic pot.

3 Slip the collar of the old plastic pot around the stem of the cucumber plant. Water well and mulch. Place an obelisk in the middle of the pot to act as support for your plant. Protect young plants from slugs and snails (see p32).

4 Help the plant up its support by regularly tying stems to the obelisk with garden twine. Keep plants well watered (see p89) and feed them regularly. Pinch back tendrils so the plant focuses its energy on flower and fruit production.

5 Harvest cucumbers at any size, by cutting each off with a sharp knife. If fruit is left to get too big it will also become less tasty and lose its texture.

Squash

It is difficult to go wrong with squash, whether they are summer or winter types. They are easy to grow, look amazing, and keep well, so you can still enjoy them long after the plants have died. Available in an incredible range of shapes, sizes, and colors, they can climb or trail. There are also compact, bushy types.

Basic needs

Grow one plant per 18in. (45cm) pot and fill it with a mix of three parts soil-based potting mix to one part well-rotted manure or garden compost. A couple of plants will fit in a grow bag.

Growing techniques

1 Sow outside in late spring or early summer, two seeds per pot, 1in. (2.5cm) deep.

2 Cover the pot with temporary row cover for

Expert tips

- Sow seeds upright, on their narrow sides, to prevent rotting.
- Leave heavier fruiting squash to trail—they are difficult to support vertically.
- If weather turns wet keep fruit off damp surfaces by placing them on old tiles.

as long as you can after germination. Thin out, leaving the strongest seedling.

3 Alternatively plant out young plants when frosts have passed. Water well.

4 Keep the soil moist, watering around the plant rather than onto it. Mulch to conserve moisture.

5 Support trailing squash with a tepee.

6 As soon as the fruit starts to swell give plants an all-purpose liquid feed every couple of weeks.

Problem solving

Protect plants, especially when young, from slugs and snails (see p32).

Harvesting and storage

Leave fruit to ripen on the plant for as long as you can and then cut with a short stem, before the frost. Listen for a hollow sound when you tap the fruit; this indicates that it is ripe. Store in a cool, dry place where the fruit will keep for several months. Seeds of squash are delicious—and nutritious too.

VARIETIES 'Baby Bear', 'Butterbush', 'Cobnut', 'Early Butternut', 'Harrier', 'Hawk', 'Hunter', 'Uchiki Kuri'

Encouraging squash to climb up a tepee, obelisk, or canes helps to keep the ripening fruit (such as this butternut squash) off damp soil in the fall.

Sweet potatoes

Actually a vine and not related to traditional potatoes at all, sweet potatoes are a great crop for pots. These rambling, clambering plants are in the soil a long time, but a pot takes up much less space and contains them nicely. Once planted sweet potato plants can be pretty much left to get on with it while you wait for the fun of harvesting. Traditionally a warm-climate crop, hardier cultivars are now available for cool-temperate areas.

Basic needs
Grow in a large container, 24in. (60cm) wide, with good drainage holes filled with a 50:50 mix of sand and all-purpose potting mix. A large, black, plastic tub is good in cool-temperate climates because it absorbs heat.

Growing techniques
1 Grow as unrooted cuttings—slips—or small transplants (see p94).

2 Pot slips into individual small pots. Water and place on a sunny windowsill until well rooted.

3 Harden before planting out into their final pots (see p95). Set them in a warm, sunny place.

4 In cool-temperate areas cover plants with temporary row covers (see p95) initially.

5 Feed every other week with an all-purpose liquid fertilizer. Water well in dry spells.

For a better crop with larger tubers give sweet potatoes some support to climb, such as a tepee of bamboo canes.

Expert tips

■ Train plants up a tepee placed over the center of the pot, helping them on with some garden twine.

■ Sweet potatoes will rot if frozen so lift tubers if frost threatens late in the season.

Problem solving
Slugs love the leaves so go on regular collecting missions at night and destroy them (see p32).

In a good summer sweet potatoes will reward you with their gorgeous blooms.

Harvesting and storage
Tubers can take up to five months to mature and are ready when the leaves turn yellow and start to die back (see p95). Skins need to harden so leave tubers somewhere warm to cure for a few days before storing in a cool, dark place. Foliage and young shoots are also tasty; pick when you require them.

VARIETIES 'Beauregard', 'Georgia Jet', 'O'Henry', 'T65'

Sweet potato bags

These attractive, scrambling vines can take over a small yard if left unchecked. Therefore they are better grown in deep, purposemade planters or bags so you can stop them rooting wherever they land. The tubers make a delicious, undemanding crop, and you can also eat the leaves and young shoots of sweet potatoes like spinach—just don't be greedy as too little foliage will reduce your harvest!

Sweet potatoes are not grown from tubers, like true potatoes, but from slips, which are cuttings, or young plants. Slips need to be grown on before planting in their final container. Therefore if you live in a cool-temperate area and young plants are available, go for these instead of slips because of the short growing season. Plant them straight into your planter. Give sweet potatoes rich, well-drained soil by mixing all-purpose potting mix with sand (see p93). This is a warm-climate crop so it needs heat to grow well and extra protection; use temporary row covers for as long as you can if temperatures are cool.

Sweet potatoes are rampant plants and will take up much less room if you train them up supports. This will also help to stop these tenacious climbers from rooting wherever their leaf nodes touch the soil, giving you a fiddly crop of lots of little tubers, rather than fewer, larger ones. Guide them back onto their canes every few weeks.

Water sweet potatoes regularly as they are thirsty plants, but don't overdo it—they hate sitting in wet soil. Give them an all-purpose liquid feed every couple of weeks.

To get a headstart next year, take stem cuttings at the end of summer and root them in water. Then pot up and overwinter them in a frost-free spot, ready for planting early next year.

Sweet potatoes are attractive, exotic-looking, scrambling plants, quite unlike traditional potatoes in appearance. Their handsome leaves can also be picked and eaten.

Planting your sweet potatoes

What you need

- sweet potato slips;
- large jar of water;
- tall pots or root trainers;
- all-purpose soilless mix;
- horticultural sand;
- potato planter
- temporary row cover;
- bamboo canes and twine.

1 Unwrap the potato slips as soon as they arrive. They may look a little wilted and tired, so place them in a jar of water overnight to revive them.

2 The next day insert the slips up to the base of the leaves into a tall pot or root trainer filled with potting mix (see p93). Water well. Grow on under cover for 2–3 weeks, until plants have established decent root systems.

3 Fill your planter with fresh all-purpose soilless mix combined with sand and plant up, spacing plants evenly around the edge. A 15-gallon planter (as here) should have space for five plants, while a pot of 20in. (50cm) diameter should hold 5–6 plants. Water well.

4 Protect young plants under temporary row cover for as long as feasible in cool-temperate areas. Feed and water regularly. After removing the cover, support each plant by erecting a tepee over the planter, with one cane for each plant to twine up (see p93).

5 Harvest crops carefully so as not to bruise the tubers and cure their skins by storing them for about 10 days in a humid, airy place. Be sure to collect your crop before the frosts, which will destroy tubers.

Potatoes

Potatoes are a crop that traditionally takes up a lot of room in the ground, but it is surprisingly successful in containers. Although the yield will not be huge, the secret with potatoes is depth, so choose your container carefully and concentrate on growing the delicious, more unusual earlies that are either unavailable in the stores or expensive when they are. Earlies are usually harvested quickly too, which means you should avoid the frustrating disappointment of late blight.

Basic needs

Potatoes will grow in just about anything that is at least 12in. (30cm) wide and deep with good drainage, including purposemade bags, large rubber tubs, and even old soil-mix bags. Grow them in all-purpose potting mix.

Harvest potatoes carefully either by upturning bags and pots or by rummaging gently with a small handfork.

Growing techniques

1 Green potatoes before planting, which means help them to presprout. To do this stand them in egg cartons or seed flats in a cool, light place, with the end bearing the most eyes upward (see p98). When shoots are around 1in. (2.5cm) long the tubers can be planted out.

2 Depending on type, plant from early spring (see p98). Place the container in a sunny spot, then fill it with 8in. (20cm) potting mix and sprinkle in a little fertilizer (see p99). Plant the presprouted tubers—two is ample for a container 12in. (30cm) in diameter—and cover with 4in. (10cm) of potting mix. Then water it.

3 As the plants grow keep covering their shoots and leaves with potting mix (see p99) until the soil almost reaches the top of the pot.

4 Potatoes need a consistent supply of water for the best harvest, so keep plants well watered, particularly while tubers are starting to develop.

5 Give a liquid feed regularly (see p98).

Problem solving

Your biggest challenge will be avoiding late blight, a fungal disease that can wipe out an entire potato crop (see p35). It flourishes in warm, wet weather and usually strikes around late summer, so the best way to beat late blight is to grow early varieties, which are out of the ground before it hits. Otherwise be vigilant; at the first sign of its

Presprouted potatoes grow well in bags. As the potato plants develop, gradually unroll the bag sides and top up the potting mix until it reaches the top of each bag.

distinctive, chocolate blotching cut leaves down to the ground to stop late blight spreading to the tubers underground. Leave the potatoes in the pot for a couple of weeks to harden their skins and hope you have a crop left. Another, much less significant problem—scab—causes marking on the skins and, although it is mainly a decorative problem and can easily be peeled off, you should not store affected potatoes.

Harvesting and storage

Earlies should be ready when in flower. They are best eaten at once, so lift only when you need them. You can start to lift mid- and long-season varieties any time after flowering. When the foliage turns yellow, cut it down; then leave tubers for a week or so to harden their skins. After lifting, dry them in the sun for a few hours. Store in the dark in breathable bags—burlap is perfect.

The later you leave potato plants the bigger the tubers will get, although the longer you leave them the greater the risk of pest or disease.

VARIETIES earlies: 'Accent', 'Riviera', 'Winston'; midseason: 'Charlotte', 'Duke of York', 'Kondor','Pixie'; long-season: 'Pink Fir Apple', 'Ratte', 'Sarpo'

Bags of potatoes

Potatoes will grow in just about anything as long as the container has enough depth, and these bright, cheery, recycled bags make easy and attractive planters. They are ideal for those who don't have much space or for growers who don't want what space they do have dominated by just one demanding crop.

In addition to recycled bags made from porous fabric, you can also plant presprouted seed potatoes in purposemade planters or use large tubs, which are easy to drill holes in yourself. Grow from early until late spring for summer crops or plant in late summer for harvests in the winter right up until Christmas. If your space is limited, go for the more flavorsome potato varieties so your harvests are really special (see p97). Look for blight-resistant varieties if fungal disease could be a problem.

Place bags in a sunny spot and feed plants every other week with specialized potato fertilizer or an all-purpose liquid one. When wanting to harvest early potatoes have a gentle feel in the bag first to establish the size of the tubers and, if they are too small, give them another week to develop.

Opposite: Make sure the potatoes are clean and dry before storing. To do this, leave harvested potatoes on the soil for a couple of hours until the soil on them is dry. The tubers will rot if stored when still damp.

Planting your potato sack

What you need
- 4 x seed potatoes per bag;
- egg carton or seed flat;
- potato planter, recycled bag, or large tub;
- all-purpose potting mix;
- specialized potato fertilizer.

1 Get your seed potatoes started by presprouting them, that is, stand them in old egg cartons or seed flats in a cool, light place. Most of the buds will be on one end, usually called the rose end, so make sure these are all facing upward.

2 In late spring or early summer plant out the presprouted potatoes. Their shoots will be 1/2–1in. (1–2.5cm) long. Add 8in. (20cm) potting mix to the bottom of the bag and work in a scoop of potato fertilizer.

3 Place the presprouted potatoes, rose ends up, in the potting mix. Then cover them with 4–8in. (10–20cm) more potting mix. Water the soil well. Fertilize them every two weeks.

4 As they grow keep adding potting mix to the bag at regular intervals, covering the shoots and leaves each time. Continue mounding until the soil is about 2in. (5cm) from the top of the bag.

5 Water the bags well in dry weather, particularly when the plants are flowering. Early potatoes are ready to harvest when in flower; mid- and long-season varieties are harvested after the foliage has started to fade (see p97).

Beet

Delicious when young and tender, beet is a healthy, versatile crop that gives you an extra harvest since the spinachlike leaves are edible too. It works well in a container, sown closely together for lots of small, sweet roots. Beet is also great as a catch crop, being sown and harvested while waiting for other crops to come up (see p102). Sow little and often for a regular supply.

Basic needs

Grow in a large container, 12–16in. (30–40cm) in diameter, filled with soil-based or all-purpose potting mix. A large container will help to hold in more moisture, which beet likes.

Growing techniques

1 Sow seed from midspring to midsummer, making regular sowings every couple of weeks.

2 Thin out seedlings regularly so they have plenty of room in which to develop.

3 Keep plants well watered, especially as the roots start to swell, and feed regularly.

Expert tips

- Don't be tempted to sow too early. Germination can be erratic—wait until midspring before starting to do so.
- Remove the leaves by twisting, rather than cutting them, to stop bleeding (see p102).

Problem solving

Choose bolt-resistant varieties if sowing early—cooler weather can cause early flowering. To stop plants running to seed keep the potting mix moist. Net plants if birds are bothersome.

Harvesting and storage

Lift when roots are the size of a golf ball and eat fresh, grated raw, or cooked, or you can pickle and store beets. Eat leaves as chard (see p113).

VARIETIES 'Action', 'Boltardy', 'Burpee's Golden', 'Cylindra', 'Moneta', 'Monodet', 'Pablo', 'Pronto', 'Red Ace', 'Solo'

The more space you give beet when you thin out young seedlings the larger the roots you will get.

Beet is one of the few crops that delivers a truly delicious double harvest—its leaves and roots are edible.

Carrots

Homegrown carrots are loaded with sweetness and they work brilliantly in pots, and you'll avoid any problems you might otherwise suffer from heavy or stony soil in open ground. You'll also be able to bamboozle carrot rust fly, by growing plants above the height at which it can fly. Finally the many short-rooted, speedy varieties mean you can dot carrots among other veg or sow a crop while you are waiting for something else to grow.

Basic needs
Grow in any container, tub, or trough 8in. (20cm) or more deep. Use all-purpose potting mix over a base layer of grit, to give carrots the light, well-drained medium that they love.

Growing techniques
1 For main-season crops sow seed from midspring to midsummer (see p105).

2 Sow thinly to reduce the amount of thinning needed later—mixing the tiny seed with sand helps and also provides extra drainage.

3 Sow short, successional rows every few weeks for a constant supply of carrots.

4 Although drought resistant, keep the plants watered to prevent woody roots. Feed regularly.

Problem solving
Carrot rust fly are drawn to the smell of crushed,

Unless harvesting a whole crop of carrots at once, avoid lifting them during the day, when carrot rust fly are around. Instead, wait until evening, when there is less chance of attack.

brushed leaves so touch plants as little as possible. Thin carrots, water, and harvest in the evening when these pests are less active.

Harvesting and storage
Dig up early varieties 12 weeks after sowing, maincrops after 16 weeks. Carrots are best eaten fresh; some can also be stored in paper sacks, in boxes of damp sand, or frozen after blanching.

VARIETIES 'Adelaide', 'Amsterdam Forcing', 'Bertan', 'Ideal', 'Maestro', 'Mignon', 'Mini Finger', 'Parmex', 'Resistafly', 'Valor'

Expert tips

- Outsmart low-flying carrot rust fly by planting in pots 2ft. (60cm) or more high; otherwise erect barriers around the plants to that height or lift up the pots.

- Maincrop varieties are the best to grow if you want crops for storing.

Beet bonanza

Beets are refreshingly simple to grow, taste delicious, and make a handsome crop in a pot with their fresh green leaves streaked with red veins and stems. When sown closely for young, sweet roots they almost burst from the pot, just asking to be picked!

There are many more beet varieties than the round, ruby-red roots we are all familiar with. There are white ones, striped ones, golden yellow ones, and long, cylindrical types. These are all grown in the same way, although it is best to choose the rounder types when growing in pots. Sow from midspring until midsummer; if you do so any earlier you may experience problems with germination. However, if you cannot wait, sow indoors in cell packs or under temporary row covers.

Sow a pot every few weeks for a successional harvest and place pots in a sunny spot, although beets do tolerate partial shade.

Most beet seeds are actually clusters of two or three, but this means they need thinning soon after germination to give the seedlings plenty of space to grow healthily. Do this by cutting surplus seedlings off with scissors, so as not to disturb the ones that are left. When seedlings reach about ¾in. (2cm) high thin them again to their final spacing of 2–4in. (5–10cm)—the closer they are spaced, the smaller the roots you will get.

When harvesting pull up individual plants by the leaves and then twist off the foliage rather than cutting it off with a knife—twisting reduces the amount of bleeding of the red beet juice. You can use the roots in a variety of ways (see p100). The young leaves go well in salads, and you can steam older leaves as you would spinach.

Beet thrives in a pot as long as it is kept watered. Water particularly thoroughly in warm, dry weather and when the roots are starting to swell.

Sowing your beet seed

What you need

- terra-cotta pot at least 8in. (20cm) in diameter and 8in. (20cm) deep;
- all-purpose or soil-based potting mix;
- drainage material such as Styrofoam chunks, gravel, or broken terra-cotta pieces (see p15);
- beet seed such as 'Moneta' or 'Barbabietola di Chioggia' (see p100);
- all-purpose liquid fertilizer.

1 Line the base with drainage material. Fill the pot with potting mix, firming it with your fingertips. Leave a 2in. (5cm) gap between the soil surface and the top of the pot.

2 Water the potting mix before sowing so the seed won't get washed about later. Sow seed thinly across the top of the potting mix. Cover them with ³⁄₄in. (2cm) of mix. After sowing, water using a water-breaker so as not to disturb the seed too much.

3 Keep the potting mix moist. Seedlings should appear within a couple of weeks. Thin them out regularly so by the time the seedlings are about ³⁄₄in. (2cm) high they are 2in. (5cm) or more apart. Keep your plants well watered and fed.

4 Harvest tender, baby roots when they are the size of golf balls, pulling them sharply by the leaves and taking care not to disturb the remaining plants. This will make room for the other roots to develop further.

Carrots and chives

Sweet, crisp carrots are one of the easiest crops to grow in a pot, as you can make the potting mix as light and free draining as these plants need and simply lift the pot onto a table so they grow well out of the way of the dreaded carrot rust fly. In the open ground, however, conditions are more exacting, and barriers are needed against this pest. Onions (*Allium*) are often used to mask the scent of carrot leaves from the carrot rust fly, so plant a row of chives (*A. schoenoprasum*) around the edge of the pot as a precaution.

Carrots are best sown directly into their final pot, because, like all root vegetables, they hate to be disturbed, and transplanting can actively damage them. Wait until temperatures start to warm up in spring as the seed won't germinate when the temperature is below 41°F (5°C), and the cooler the temperature the paler and smaller any carrot roots will be. Place the pot in a warm, sheltered spot and make sure it is kept well watered for optimum germination. Sowing a pot such as this every three weeks or so will ensure a steady supply throughout summer rather than one huge glut of roots.

In the constant battle against plant pests and diseases it is always a good idea to grow crops with others if you can, rather than on their own as a monoculture. When alliums, such as onions, garlic, and chives, are grown with carrots, it is thought by many that their strong oniony smell masks the scent of the carrot leaves, and thus the crop may escape the attentions of carrot rust fly. Also, by growing chives alongside carrots there is the bonus of an extra crop with an oniony punch to add to salads or early potatoes. Chives' edible flowers (see p140) are also adored by bees and will help to attract these helpful pollinators to your yard (see p24).

Carrots and chives are an ideal combination. As the chives are perennial and can stay in the pot, you need to resow only the carrots for a constant supply in the growing season.

Planting your carrots & chives

What you need

- chive plant;
- glazed terra-cotta pot 8in. (20cm) or more in diameter;
- horticultural grit for drainage;
- all-purpose potting mix;
- carrot seed;
- horticultural sand.

1 Water the chives in their pot. Then remove the plant from its pot and divide it into smaller sections so that you have enough to spread around the new pot. Do this by carefully splitting the plant with your fingers, initially in half and then in half or thirds again.

2 Line the base of the pot with plenty of grit. Then fill it two thirds full with potting mix. Space the chive sections evenly around the edge of the pot and fill around them with potting mix. Top up the pot with more potting mix to about 2in. (5cm) below the rim.

3 Water the potting mix. Then mix the carrot seed with sand and scatter it thinly over the bare soil surface. Sprinkle potting mix thinly over the seed. Keep the soil moist to aid seed germination. These plants are fairly drought resistant, but keep an eye on watering if conditions are very dry.

4 Give the new carrots room by harvesting a few when very young (see p101). These can be eaten whole in salads. Pick the chive leaves when required, and harvest the remaining carrots once they are larger.

Parsnips

Parsnips require a bit of patience. Germination can be tricky and they are slow to grow, but once they get going they are easy. Either dedicate a pot to them and forget about them or sow between their rows with intercrops of quicker vegetables such as radishes and lettuces. Parsnips can be left in the ground until needed, while frost helpfully turns their starches to sugars. Do not leave them too long though—they'll turn woody and tasteless.

Basic needs

Grow only in large pots, troughs, or tubs, 16in. (40cm) or more deep, because parsnips need depth and room for their leafy growth. Mix one part sand with three parts soil-based or all-purpose potting mix.

Growing techniques

1 Sow three seeds at 10in. (25cm) intervals but do not sow too early—sowings in late winter are more likely to fail than those in spring.

2 When seedlings are ³⁄₄in. (2cm) high, thin to one seedling every 6in. (15cm).

3 Water well, keeping the potting mix moist to prevent roots from splitting. Feed regularly.

Problem solving

Thanks to canker-resistant cultivars parsnips should be trouble-free.

Harvesting and storage

Parsnips are ready to be dug up when the leaves start to die down in mid- and late winter, although traditionally you harvest after the first frost and continue pulling as you need them through the winter. Peel and cook fresh parsnips; otherwise peel, cut, and blanch before freezing.

VARIETIES 'Albion', 'Arrow', 'Dagger', 'Gladiator', 'Lancer', 'Tender and True'

Parsnips are ready to lift from midsummer onward, or may be left in the pot until needed. The longer they remain in the soil the greater the risk of attack by carrot rust fly.

Expert tips

- Parsnip seed does not retain its viability so use fresh seed every year.

- If eager to sow in late winter first warm the soil with temporary row covers and leave on until the seedlings are well established.

Radishes

Nothing is quicker or easier to grow than radishes—they are a veg garden favorite for good reason! There are crisp, sweet summer varieties ready to harvest in less than a month, and larger, hardier winter types sown toward the end of the summer. Sow summer ones in batches regularly, either in dedicated pots or dotted wherever there's space among other crops, such as parsnips.

Basic needs
Grow summer types in pots 4in. (10cm) deep, winter ones in pots 8in. (20cm) deep, filled with soil-based or all-purpose potting mix.

Growing techniques
1 Sow from early spring until late summer in an open, sunny site. Summer varieties can cope with some shade.

2 Sow summer types thinly; space seed for winter types 8in. (20cm) apart.

3 Keep potting mix moist and feed regularly.

Expert tips

■ For an early crop warm the soil under temporary row covers before sowing.

■ Sow summer varieties thinly—about 1in. (2.5cm) apart—and there should then be no need to thin the seedlings.

Problem solving
Flea beetles can do a lot of damage, peppering the leaves of young seedlings with tiny holes (see p35). It's best to net plants. Slugs and snails can decimate a young crop unless controlled (see p32). Ensure the soil does not dry out to prevent radishes from splitting or bolting.

Harvesting and storage
Summer types are best picked young and eaten right away. Lift winter varieties as you need them or harvest before the frosts and store. For edible pods let plants flower and pick the pods when crisp and green.

VARIETIES 'Amethyst', 'Cherry Belle', 'French Breakfast', 'Munchen Bier', 'Ping Pong', 'Pink Beauty', 'Rougette', 'Sparkler', 'Zlata'

Either thin radishes to give roots room to grow, or thin plants later by harvesting very young, bite-sized roots.

Radishes have a tasty, peppery punch. Munch them freshly harvested from the pot or toss them chopped into salads.

Leeks

Leeks are one of the great winter vegetables and not difficult to grow if you get a few things right. For pots there are special varieties that can be harvested early, when still small, or be left to grow on to develop into ordinary leeks.

Basic needs

Mix 1:3 parts organic matter and potting mix in a large pot, 8in. (20cm) or more deep. Avoid grow bags because they are too shallow for leeks. Baby types can have slightly smaller pots.

Growing leeks in a raised bed or large pot will give you a reasonable harvest whenever you are ready for it.

Growing techniques

1 In spring sow leek seed 4–6in. (10–15cm) apart in their final pots. Do not worry about transplanting as you would if growing them in the open ground. Sow a row of baby leeks, 1¼in. (3cm) apart, every few weeks during the growing season.

2 Leave room in the top of the pot and gradually fill it up as the leeks grow to blanch the stems.

3 Water leeks in very dry weather.

4 Topdress plants with high-nitrogen fertilizer from mid- to late summer.

Problem solving

Leeks suffer from the usual onion family problem of rust, although it should be only cosmetic. Rust is caused by wet and poor air circulation, so do not overcrowd pots.

Harvesting and storage

Harvest baby leeks when they are the thickness of a pencil, lifting them as required. Dig up maincrop leeks from the fall onward and eat them fresh. There's no need to store them because they can remain in the ground until the following spring, if you have any left!

VARIETIES 'Apollo', 'Atal', 'Imperial Summer', 'Kajak', 'King Richard', 'Longbow', Mammoth Pot', 'Musselburgh', 'Oarsman', Swiss Giant Group, 'Zermatt', 'Toledo', 'Tornado'

Expert tips

- When drawing soil up around the stems to blanch them, try not to let the soil fall in-between the leaves.
- If leek moth is a problem in your area cover young plants to stop adult moths laying their eggs in the leaves.

Onions & shallots

Onions are cheap to buy, readily available, and take a long time to grow, so concentrate your growing skills on less common, sweet red onions, mellow shallots, and lively scallions (see p110). Plant a short row or two in a large tub or dot them among other crops. Shallots will give you a bigger crop of smaller bulbs, and scallions even more—they are also an ideal catch crop.

Basic needs

For a reasonable-sized crop use a large container 8in. (20cm) or more deep. For extra nutrients add specialized onion fertilizer to a mix of soil-based potting mix and grit (see p111).

Growing techniques

1 Although onion seed is available, it is easier and quicker to grow all but scallions from sets (immature bulbs). Plant from early to midspring, 4in. (10cm) apart, or in early fall for overwintering. Ensure the pointed end of each onion set is uppermost and the tip just showing. Then water. Sow scallions at intervals from early spring for a supply through the summer.

2 Onions will bolt if they are not given enough water so mulch to conserve moisture and do not let the soil dry out. Feed plants regularly.

A simple box of scallions will give you a quick, onion tang to add to all sorts of dishes.

Dry onions in the sun for a couple of weeks to help cure their skins. They will then be ready to store.

Problem solving

Damp, humid, overcrowded conditions can cause fungal diseases such as rust and onion downy mildew, although neither should be devastating. Avoid watering foliage and ensure good light and air around plants.

Harvesting and storage

Scallions should be ready 8–10 weeks after sowing. Onions and shallots are both ready to harvest when foliage turns yellow and floppy. Leave them for 2–3 weeks and then carefully lift them with a handfork. Dry them in the sun before storing in bags or trays in a cool, dry place; they will keep for several months. Use fall-planted onions right away.

VARIETIES onion: 'Marco', 'Red Baron', 'Setton'; scallion: 'Apache', 'Lilia', 'Ramrod', 'White Lisbon'; shallot: 'Delvad', 'Eschalote Grise', 'Longor', 'Matador', 'Pikant'

Expert tip

■ Before planting remove loose skin from each onion set to stop birds pecking at it.

Onion quarters

Onions are one of the most versatile vegetables in the kitchen—you can easily find a use for an onion, shallot, or scallion every single day. Although you won't be able to grow enough for this in pots, they are a fun and easy crop to cultivate. They make an unusual container display with their upright, glaucous leaf spikes, and in this project look particularly striking against the matt black of a recycled tire tub.

In a limited space go for a few choice red onions, unusual, expensive-in-the-stores shallots, and a sprinkling of scallions, sown successionally to keep you going through the summer. A late summer sowing of scallions will be ready to pull again the following spring. Add garlic chives for a gentle tang, which can be snipped right up until the fall. Onion and shallot sets can be planted in the fall or early to midspring, depending on variety. Plant the sets in free-draining potting mix and give them a sunny, sheltered spot. All onions hate sitting in the wet and will quickly rot if they do, so adding grit to the container is a good idea. Stop watering once onions have swollen. They are ready to lift once their leaves begin to yellow, as are shallots; leave them to dry in the sun for a couple of days before using or storing (see p109). Scallions can be ready in as little as eight weeks after sowing.

Above: Harvest scallions by pulling them gently by the stems when they are about pencil thickness. They are best eaten fresh—they give a delicious, tangy punch to a salad.

Left: Resist the temptation to overplant your tub, because onions will suffer from fungal diseases if there isn't good air circulation between the plants.

Planting your mixed onion tub

What you need

- recycled tire tub;
- drill;
- horticultural grit;
- soil-based potting mix;
- specialized onion fertilizer;
- horticultural sand;
- onion and shallot sets, young garlic chive plant, scallion seed.

1 Make some drainage holes in the base of the recycled tire tub with a drill. Then line the base of the tub with a generous layer of grit. Fill the tub two thirds full with potting mix and some fertilizer and then add more grit until it is almost at the top of the tub—leave a gap of 2–4in. (5–10cm) for watering.

2 Mix the grit evenly into the potting soil and firm down with your fingers. Then using sand mark out four sections. Push the onion and shallot sets gently into the soil—each in a marked area. Ensure their tips are poking just above the surface and water them in.

3 Plant young garlic chives in spring and sow scallion seed thinly, giving each crop a dedicated quarter section of its own. Water them in.

4 Always label the crops to aid identification especially as these crops look similar. Every 10–14 days once plants are established topdress with the onion fertilizer and water it in. Water regularly while in growth.

5 Shallots should be ready from mid- to late summer when the leaves begin to flop and yellow (see p109). Leave them for 2–3 weeks before lifting. Dry in the sun for a couple of days then use at once or store them.

Garlic

By growing your own garlic you can try a whole world of new and exciting varieties. There are two basic types: soft neck, which has bendy stems that are easily braided, produces lots of small cloves, and stores well; and hard neck, which has a hard flower spike running through the middle and bears much bigger cloves. Both types pretty much look after themselves while in growth, and thrive in pots on their own or dotted among other veg.

Basic needs
Grow in a large pot, 16in. (40cm) wide, filled with equal parts soil-based potting mix, grit, and garden compost.

Garlic is best planted in late fall or early winter; in Europe it has always been traditional to plant sets by the shortest day of the year in December.

Once lifted, dry garlic in the sun for a couple of days, before storing indoors, somewhere cool.

Expert tips

- If a plant starts to flower, just snip off its head to focus the plant's energies into producing a large bulb.
- Bulbs may start sprouting and can rot in storage if you delay harvesting.
- Do not bother planting supermarket cloves—you are likely to be disappointed. They are prone to viruses and come from more tender varieties.

Growing techniques
1 Break up the bulbs and plant each clove just below the potting mix surface. Water well. A spot of cold weather will help bulbs develop.

2 Water garlic in very dry spells but take care not to overdo it. Stop watering when the foliage starts to turn yellow, which means the bulbs are reaching maturity.

Problem solving
Cover plants with floating row cover to stop birds pecking at the cloves. Long spells of wet weather may cause rust or onion rot. Do not crowd plants to help air circulate freely around them.

Harvesting and storage
Lift bulbs for green garlic in early summer or when leaves turn yellow for more mature bulbs. You can also pick young green leaves earlier for salads. Hard-neck garlic has fancy, looping flowerheads that can be snapped off and eaten. Lift bulbs with a handfork and store in old vegetable crates or braid soft-neck garlic stems and hang in the cool to dry.

VARIETIES soft-neck: 'Arno', 'Cristo', 'Early Purple Wight', 'Solent Wight', 'Spring Wight'; hard-neck: 'Early Wight', 'Lautrec'

Chard

Chard is one of the most ornamental crops and looks fantastic in pots, particularly if you choose one of the varieties with colored stems such as 'Bright Lights' or vibrant pink-stemmed 'Rhubarb Chard'. It is difficult to fail with this crop, and it is brilliantly hardy, often lasting right through the winter until it is time to sow a new crop the following spring.

Basic needs

Plants need a pot 8in. (20cm) or more deep since they have long taproots, so choose a large container or trough rather than a grow bag. Use all-purpose or soil-based potting mix, but add a couple of trowelfuls of garden compost or manure to the bottom of the pot to feed the chard roots.

Growing techniques

1 In midspring sow seed thinly, 1in. (2.5cm) deep. Place the pot in an open site that is preferably sunny. If you have the space sow again in midsummer for crops that can be harvested the following spring.

2 Mulch to conserve water and do not let the potting mix dry out. Feed regularly.

3 Plants may need protection with straw and floating row covers in cool-temperate areas during winter.

Problem solving

Chard is a toughie and usually trouble-free.

Harvesting and storage

Start to harvest leaves and stems just 10 weeks after sowing. Pick often and when needed to keep new leaves coming, cutting outer leaves first when these are young and tender. Chard keeps for a few days in the refrigerator, but it does not freeze well.

Chard is a distinctive, ornamental plant that keeps on developing edible leaves and stems for use as and when you need them.

Expert tips

- If plants are left to flower the flower stalks can be cooked and eaten in the same way as sprouting broccoli.
- Although chard tolerates some shade you will get a better crop in full sun.

VARIETIES 'Bright Lights', 'Bright Yellow', 'Canary Yellow', 'Charlotte', 'Costa Bianca', 'Fordhook Giant', 'Lucullus', 'Rhubarb Chard'

Spinach

Delicious, nutritious spinach can be picked as small, tender, cut-and-come-again leaves for salads or be allowed to grow bushier for larger leaves for cooking. It grows year-round so is a handy crop to have in a pot when other greens are in short supply. New Zealand spinach, although not a true spinach, tastes almost the same and romps happily through hot summers, when traditional spinach bolts.

Basic needs
Use soil-based potting mix with slow-release fertilizer and grit in a pot 8in. (20cm) deep.

Growing techniques
1 Sow thinly every couple of weeks from early spring to early fall, depending on the variety.

2 Place the pot in a slightly shady spot or grow plants among taller crops so the spinach is kept cool and the potting mix does not dry out too quickly.

3 Thin seedlings only for large-leaved crops.

4 Keep plants watered well and feed regularly.

5 Winter crops may need protection.

Problem solving
They are usually trouble-free apart from attacks on seedlings by slugs and snails (see p32). Plants may bolt if the potting mix is dry.

Expert tips

- Spinach bolts very easily, so stop sowing from early summer, when dry weather can cause problems. Sow winter varieties at the end of the summer.

- To stop leaves tasting bitter make sure the potting mix has plenty of fertilizer or garden compost added at planting time.

Harvesting and storage
Keep cutting leaves as soon as they are big enough to use, to encourage further growth. Eat right away; do not bother freezing spinach.

VARIETIES 'Bordeaux', 'Dominant', 'Emilia', 'Lazio', 'Matador', 'Mikado', 'Scenic', 'Toscane'; New Zealand spinach

Sow spinach earlier in the season rather than later to prevent it from bolting, which it does readily in hot, dry weather.

Harvest the fresh, young leaves of spinach for use in mixed salads and sandwiches or lightly steam them in stir-fries.

Rhubarb

Rhubarb is an impressive-looking plant. Although it needs a large container, it is perfectly feasible to grow it in such a restricted environment. You can even get bag kits for rhubarb. It is easy and undemanding; copes well with neglect; and is completely hardy and perennial so it will last a long time. Rhubarb also crops over a long period especially if given a little extra assistance.

Basic needs
Grow each rhubarb crown in a large pot, 24in. (60cm) wide and deep, with plenty of drainage holes—old garbage cans are ideal.

Growing techniques
1 The best plants are grown from young crowns or divided from mature ones.

2 Plant from midfall to late winter with the growing point at or just below the potting mix surface (see p117). Water plants well.

3 Set the pot in a sunny, frost-free spot.

4 Mulch in spring with well-rotted organic matter to retain moisture, taking care not to bury the crown. Water and feed the plant regularly.

5 Allow the foliage to die back in the fall. Then remove it to expose the growing point to the winter cold.

Problem solving
Look out for limp leaves and weak growth, which is indicative of the fungal disease crown rot. Dig up and trash affected plants.

Harvesting and storage
Pull stems with a twisting motion (see p116), rather than cutting, so you do not leave behind a stump, which will rot. Harvest only half the stems in one go, from spring until midsummer. For an early harvest of pink, tender stems, force plants in mid- to late winter by covering them with straw and an upturned bucket or garbage can lid.

Rhubarb can be eaten raw, cooked, or frozen when cooked.

VARIETIES 'Hawke's Champagne', 'Raspberry Red', 'Timperley Early', 'Victoria'

Expert tips

■ Remove any flowerheads as they appear.

■ Do not harvest rhubarb in its first season, and pick only lightly the second year after planting to avoid weakening crowns.

■ If forcing rhubarb in spring leave the plant to recover for the rest of the season. You can crop from it again the following year.

■ Divide plants after five years, splitting the crown into sections with a spade.

Rhubarb adds an exotic touch with its large, leathery leaves and ruby stems. Remove tired leaves so the plant looks fresh.

Rhubarb for picking

This handsome crop looks fantastic in a pot, adding a certain lushness to a shady spot. Rhubarb needs a big container however, and old garbage cans are particularly suitable especially when attractively painted as shown here.

Rhubarb is best grown from young crowns planted between midfall and late winter, although you will need to exert a little patience, because you can't harvest plants in the first year. Otherwise rhubarb doesn't ask for much—just give it food and water and the subsequent harvests will be well worth the wait. It's a deep-rooting plant, which is why garbage cans are good, but a single crown will happily grow in a large pot, 24in. (60cm) wide and deep. Rhubarb is quite a greedy plant so give it a generous helping of organic matter when planting and keep it well watered in summer. Mulching the plant in spring will also help retain water in the soil (see p115). Rhubarb hates sitting in cold, wet soil so do not give plants any extra water over winter. As a leafy crop rhubarb requires a nitrogen feed rather than a liquid 5–5–10 one for fruiting crops, so give it a boost in spring by feeding it with a slow-release fertilizer. Plants also need a frosty winter to produce the best stalks so remove the dead foliage once it has died back to expose the crown to the cold.

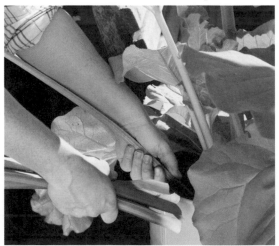

Above: Harvest rhubarb by pulling the stalks any time between late spring and the end of summer, taking just a few at a time so as not to weaken the plant.

Right: Rhubarb grows well in any large, deep, well-drained container, such as a garbage can. Be sure to water your plant well during any prolonged periods of dry, summer weather.

Planting your rhubarb

What you need
- masking tape and drill;
- garbage can;
- drainage material (see p15);
- soil-based potting mix;
- well-rotted manure or garden compost;
- rhubarb crown.

1 Space strips of tape evenly around the bottom of the garbage can to stop your drill from slipping, then drill holes through the base. Line the bottom of the garbage can with drainage material.

2 Mix together two parts of potting mix to one part well-rotted manure or garden compost. Fill the bin about three quarters full with the soil mixture.

3 Plant the rhubarb crown, taking care not to set it too deeply—the growing tip should be at or just below the surface of the potting mix.

4 Water well to help the plant establish and mulch, but take care not to bury the crown of the rhubarb. Feed and water regularly in the growing season. Keep plants dry in winter. Mulch the plant again each spring; do it after watering to help retain moisture.

5 Leave the rhubarb to establish during its first growing season and pick only a few stems in the second year (see p115).

Bush & pole beans

Beans are one of the prettiest, easiest, and most prolific crops you can grow. They are practically self sufficient and so rewarding it is almost exhausting keeping up with them, so do not grow too many! Not only are they great for novice growers but they also look fantastic trained up a tepee in a pot.

Basic needs

Beans are hungry so need equal parts of well-rotted manure and soil-based potting mix. Use as big a pot as you can: at least 8in. (20cm) deep and 2ft. (60cm) wide for pole beans; 6in. (15cm) deep and 12in. (30cm) wide for bush beans.

Growing techniques

1 Beans are sensitive to cold so wait to sow outside until late spring or early summer.

2 Place the pot in a warm, sunny, sheltered spot.

3 Support vining beans (except dwarf varieties) with a tepee, canes, or trellis and help the young plants by tying stems in loosely to the support until they can climb by themselves (see p121).

4 Keep the potting mix moist at all times, and mulch at the beginning of summer to conserve moisture.

5 Feed plants every week in summer with a liquid 5–5–10 fertilizer (see p125).

Problem solving

Slugs and snails love the young seedlings so deter them (see p32). Any armies of aphids in early summer can be squished by hand (see p34), and planting marigolds in the pot is said to help deter aphids. Use fresh potting mix every year to avoid foot and root rot fungal disease.

Birds can peck at pole bean flowers, although they find white ones less attractive than red blooms.

Harvesting and storage

Pick pole beans when 6–8in. (15–20cm) long and before you see beans swelling inside. Bush beans are ready when 4in. (10cm) long. Both can be blanched and frozen, pickled, or made into chutney. Half-ripe bush beans can be eaten fresh or dried. Bush beans mature into kidney and lima beans, which can be dried and stored.

VARIETIES borlotti: 'Borlotto Lingua di Fuoco'; dwarf bush: 'Golddukat', 'Maja', 'Purple Teepee', 'Safari', 'Speedy', 'The Prince'; dwarf runner: 'Hestia', 'Pickwick'; pole: 'Celebration', 'Red Flame'; vining bush: 'Cobra'

'Hestia' is a dwarf, bushy variety that has been bred specifically for growing in pots and containers.

Expert tips

- Lack of moisture causes poor crops, so water regularly and well.
- Mist pole-bean flowers to help them set.
- The more you pick the more beans a plant produces, so keep at it.

Fava beans

Fava beans are an old favorite in the veg garden, a delicious staple that is easy to grow in pots, especially if you choose one of the dwarf varieties that reach half the height of the others. All fava beans are lovely picked young, tender, and sweet and simply must be homegrown to get them at their best.

Basic needs
Fava beans have long taproots so need a pot 8in. (20cm) or more deep with good drainage. A large pot, 2ft. (60cm) in diameter, is best for a decent crop. Use soil-based potting mix.

Growing techniques
1 Hardy varieties can be sown in the fall, otherwise the main sowing time is early to late spring.

2 Sow seed 2in. (5cm) deep, 6–8in. (15–20cm) apart. Place the pot in full sun.

3 Support taller plants with canes and twine or with peasticks, as they develop.

4 Keep the potting mix moist at all times. Water especially well as soon as plants start to flower, and feed regularly.

Problem solving
Chocolate spot may appear on the leaves of plants grown too close together, in damp, humid weather. It is mainly a cosmetic problem, as are the distinctive leaf notches made by pea and bean weevils. Mice love digging up the fat seeds, so cover the pots until the seed germinates. Also protect young shoots against slugs (see p32). Remove black bean aphids by hand (see p34).

Harvesting and storage
Fava beans can be eaten at all stages, from small, slender pods to fat beans that need shelling and peeling. Pick regularly and eat fresh, or freeze after blanching.

Expert tips

- Stay one step ahead of aphids by sowing in the fall; in cool-temperate areas protect plants with temporary row covers in winter.

- Pinch back the top 3in. (7.5cm) of plants as soon as pods start to form. It diverts energy into the pods and removes the part of the plant that the black bean aphid loves. (The tops are delicious steamed and buttered, so do not throw them away.)

Unlike most fava beans, which are tall and have a tendency to topple over, 'Robin Hood' is a compact variety ideal for growing in containers. Sow in the fall for an early crop.

VARIETIES 'Aquadulce Claudia', 'Crimson Flowered', 'Express', 'Jubilee Hysor', 'Karmazyn', 'Medes', 'Optica', 'Robin Hood', 'The Sutton'

Beans & sunflowers

Pole beans and sunflowers are some of the most rewarding crops to grow together, demanding only a regular supply of water in exchange for beautiful flowers and generous supplies of beans. Together they make a stunning combination and work really well in this large, square granite pot. They also provide a great project for children, who love sowing the large seed and watching these fun crops grow in summer.

Sow this pot when the frosts have passed, in a sunny, sheltered spot. Spot sow the seed, planting two at a time in case any fail, and leave at least 4in. (10cm) between the sunflower and the bean seeds so that they have plenty of

room to develop. Six plants of each should grow together quite happily in a pot 16in. (40cm) wide.

It seems that beans prefer to climb up sunflowers rather than bamboo canes—maybe the hairy plant stems are a better grip for them than those of smooth bamboo. However it is a good idea to support the sunflowers with canes in case they get overwhelmed by the beans. The beans can use the canes as well. Use smaller canes when the plants first start growing and then replace them with taller ones at least the final height of the sunflowers when they reach the top of the cane. If the odd bean ventures onto one of the first, smaller canes gently guide it back to the sunflower stem. Once the taller canes are in place beans can be left to scramble up them. When they reach the top of either the sunflowers or the canes, nip off their tips to stop them growing farther and to keep them cropping well. Regular watering for both of these thirsty crops is vital, particularly when the beans are in flower or the young pods are developing.

Harvest the petals of the sunflowers for salads as the flowers open and leave the seeds to dry on the plant, either for yourself or the birds. Keep picking the beans—the more you do so the more they will continue to produce new beans until the frosts in the fall (see p118).

This dazzling pot is simple to grow, looks stunning, and is extremely productive, providing the grower with a seemingly endless amount of beans at the same time as wowing them with beautiful flowers.

Planting your beans & sunflowers

What you need

- square granite pot, 16in. (40cm) or more in diameter;
- drainage material (see p15);
- soil-based potting mix;
- bean and sunflower seed;
- bamboo canes—short and long;
- garden twine.

1 Line the bottom of the pot with drainage material and fill with potting mix, leaving a 2in. (5cm) gap between the rim and the potting mix. Moisten the potting mix. Spot sow each crop, two seeds at a time for insurance. Then water.

2 Nip off the weaker seedlings at each spot after germination. As the plants develop insert canes into the potting mix as support for the sunflowers. Tie them in with garden twine. Mulch with garden compost (see p118).

3 If by chance a lone bean does start to climb up a short cane, gently guide it back onto the sunflower stem.

4 Once the sunflowers reach the tops of the short canes, replace these with taller ones to ensure the sunflowers have support when the beans start to get heavy. Tie them in well. Mist the bean flowers to aid setting if necessary.

5 Keep these thirsty plants well watered, especially when flowers appear; this may mean watering morning and night in hot weather. Also feed regularly. Nip off the growing tips of the beans when they reach the tops of their supports.

Peas

Homegrown peas are a must for any pot. Their sugars start turning to starch the second they are picked, so it is only by growing your own that you can truly taste fresh peas at their best. The shoots and tips are also delicious in salads—you could even grow pots of peas just for the shoots. And give snow peas and snap peas a try; although tall they are quicker-growing than garden peas.

Basic needs
Grow in a pot 8in. (20cm) or more deep, although some container varieties such as 'Half Pint' will crop in a window box. They need good drainage, so choose soil-based potting mix and a container with plenty of drainage holes.

Growing techniques
1 Sow wrinkly and round-seeded peas from early spring to early summer, 4in. (10cm) apart. Round seed is hardier and can also be sown in the fall. Spread the sowing over a few weeks to avoid any gluts.

For a long, steady supply of sweet, fresh peas, keep picking the plump pods to encourage more to develop.

2 Place the container in an open, sunny spot.

3 Taller pea varieties need something to scramble up—twiggy peasticks, bamboo canes, or netting will help them to cling and climb (see p127).

4 Keep an eye on watering, especially after flowering. Young pods need lots of moisture to swell fully. Feed the plants regularly.

Problem solving
Use netting or start plants off indoors to protect them against birds, which tear at leaves and destroy young seedlings, and mice, which can eat the seed before it even has a chance to germinate. Avoid burrowing caterpillars of the pea moth in midsummer by sowing early and late. Do not worry too much about leaf notches left by pea and bean weevils since they should not affect your crop.

Harvesting and storage
Most peas are ready within a couple of months of sowing, when pods are full. Pick snow peas and snap peas just as the peas are developing; eat the pods whole. Pod garden peas and eat them raw or cook or freeze straightaway.

VARIETIES 'Balmoral', 'Greensage', 'Half Pint', 'Kelvedon Wonder', 'Misty', 'Purple Podded', 'Serge'; snap peas: 'Cascadia', 'Sugar Ann'; snow peas: 'Oregon Giant', 'Oregon Sugarpod'

Sweet corn

Corn can be tricky in pots because it is wind-pollinated and needs to be grown in blocks to maximize pollination. However if you have pots that are big enough, it is definitely worthwhile. Mini varieties are perfect for smaller containers—they are harvested before pollination even occurs. The only way to appreciate sweet corn at its absolute best is to grow your own, since its sugars start turning to starch as soon as it is picked.

Basic needs
Grow five or six traditional corn plants in a very large pot or tub, 8in. (20cm) or more deep and 2ft. (60cm) or more in diameter. Minis can grow in a slightly smaller pot. Bag kits are also available. Give corn rich soil by combining three parts potting mix with one part garden compost or organic matter.

Growing techniques
1 Corn needs warmth for germination so sow indoors or under glass. Sow outside once temperatures reach 50°F (10°C) and frosts have definitely passed; or grow from young plants.

2 Plant traditional corn varieties in groups of at least five plants so they can pollinate each other. Place the pots in a sunny, sheltered spot.

3 Ensure the pots are kept well watered and fed. Corn plants are thirsty, especially when in pots.

Problem solving
Usually trouble-free.

Harvesting and storage
Pick mini types just before the tassels

Start corn under cover in midspring, or sow outside once frosts have passed.

Newer varieties of sweet corn, known as supersweet, have even higher levels of sugar than traditional ones. 'Sweetie Pie' is an early maturing variety that is exceptionally sweet.

appear. Traditional sweet corn is ready when the tassels turn rusty brown and the kernels release a creamy sap—test with your thumbnail (see p124). Twist cobs off the stem just before you eat them; otherwise keep the leaves on the cobs and get them in the refrigerator quickly. Kernels can be cut off, blanched, and frozen. Hang popping corn types up to dry before popping.

VARIETIES 'Minor', 'Mirai', 'Sundance', 'Swallow', 'Sweetie Pie', 'Swift'; mini corn: 'Minipop'; popping corn: 'Strawberry Popcorn'

Expert tips

- Mulch plants to keep in moisture and mound potting mix up over any exposed roots for stability.
- Watering is vital when plants are in flower. Apply liquid feed when cobs start to swell.
- Help pollination by tapping the tassels when they appear.
- Grow only one type of corn in a small space; if mixed, they cross-pollinate and the flavor is reduced.

Beans & sweet corn

Inspired by the American Indian method of companion planting, this large, plastic tub holds elegant canes of corn and dwarf pole beans. In the original system, the beans climb up the corn, but here the bushy habit of the beans provides a living mulch around the base of the corn, keeping the roots cool, the canes stable, and the potting mix moist.

For drainage material in such a large pot it is a good idea to reuse plastic plant pots rather than lots of pottery shards or gravel. Such pots are light and will easily fill the bottom of the tub, reducing the amount of potting mix needed and making the planter easier to move around if you need to. Traditionally corn is grown in blocks rather than rows to help pollination (see p123), so as long as your tub is large enough to give plants room to grow they should crop well grouped together in

a pot. Next to each cane plant a dwarf pole bean. The flowers are edible as well as the pods. Be sure to keep on picking the beans as they develop— leaving them on the plant will stop production and shorten your harvest.

Sow seed directly in late spring or early summer, when all danger of frosts has passed. Place the tub in a bright, sunny spot, out of the wind, so that pollinating insects can easily reach the bean flowers. Water these crops well, particularly when they are in flower and when the pods and cobs are developing. Give them a regular weekly liquid 5–5–10 feed from this point onward. Mulch around plants in summer (see p118).

Above: Cobs are ready when the tassels turn a rusty brown. Test them for ripeness by sticking a thumbnail in a kernel. If a milky sap is released it is ripe; if it is still clear, leave the cob on the plant for another day or two.

Left: The combination of corn and beans grown together in one pot works really well, with the beans providing nitrogen and protection for the corn. The corn will support the beans and shelter them, and so encourage bees and other pollinating insects to the flowers.

Planting your beans & corn

What you need
■ large, plastic tub 20in. (50cm) in diameter;
■ drainage material (see p15) or old plastic plant pots;
■ soil-based potting mix;
■ sweet corn and dwarf pole bean seed.

1 Line the bottom of this large pot with old plastic plant pots or a generous layer of drainage material.

2 Cover the pots with potting mix, filling the tub only to 2in. (5cm) below the rim, to leave room for watering. Water the potting mix.

3 Spot sow two corn seeds at each spot to ensure sufficient plants if some fail to germinate. Six or seven plants will fit well in a pot this size, spaced evenly around the sides and across the middle.

4 Sow the bean seed in exactly the same way, two seeds per spot, close to the corn so that they will be conveniently placed to grow up each corn stem. Water well. Thin out the weaker seedling of each crop in each spot.

5 Water and feed the plants regularly. Both corn and beans are thirsty plants and may need watering twice a day in hot weather, morning and evening. Eat sweet corn as soon as it is harvested (see p123) and pick beans regularly (see p118).

A summer pot

If you want to try just a few crops for the summer this is a quick and easy combination that will keep you in fresh veg over a number of weeks. The crisp romaine should be ready within eight weeks from sowing, followed by the peas, twining up through the center, while the ruby-red beet can be picked as soon as it reaches golf-ball size.

Romaine, with its narrow, upright habit, is a good choice in a limited space. Go for any round beet variety, rather than a cylindrical type, which may struggle at the edge of a pot. Any garden, snap, or snow pea variety could be used in this planting.

Sow your seed directly in the final pot in late spring, placing it in an open, sunny spot. Don't be tempted to sow earlier than this, because pea seed can rot in cold, damp soil. Water the potting mix before sowing and, to save time thinning lots of seedlings later on, spot sow the seed exactly where you want each plant to grow. Give the pot a feed with an all-purpose liquid fertilizer every two weeks and keep it well watered, especially once the peas are in flower. When the pea seedlings emerge nip off the weakest one of each pair so that there is just one plant per cane.

The lettuces will be ready when each has developed a good, firm head (see p131). Harvest the first few beet when they are baby roots (see p100), and this will give the remaining ones the space to develop into a bigger size if you wish. Keep picking the peas regularly so they are absolutely fresh, harvesting them from the bottom of the plant upward (see p122).

All the crops in this pot can be succession sown in other pots, two or three weeks after these, for a continuous supply of delicious, fresh food.

Planting your summer pot

What you need

- terra-cotta pot 16in. (40cm) or more in diameter;
- drainage material (see p15);
- soil-based potting mix;
- bamboo canes;
- garden twine;
- pea, beet, and romaine seed.

1 Line the bottom of the pot with drainage material and then top up with potting mix to about 2in. (5cm) below the rim. Firm the potting mix. Arrange the canes evenly in a circle half way across the pot, leaving space for the beet and lettuces to grow around the edge.

2 Bring the tops of the canes together and secure them with twine, winding it around and around before making a knot.

3 Before sowing, water the potting mix so that it is moist. Sow two pea seeds at the base of each cane, followed by a pinch of lettuce seed and a row of beet seed around the edge of the pot. Keep the potting mix moist while the seed germinates.

4 Thin out the beet (see p100) and lettuce seedlings to allow room for the rest to mature. Help the young pea plants up the canes until they can start to cling and twine by themselves. Feed and water plants regularly.

5 Pick the pea pods regularly so they are always young and fresh. Harvest each lettuce when it has a good head, and the beets at whatever size you like them.

Cabbages

There are so many cabbage varieties that you could keep a harvest going through the year, but for container growing it is advisable to stick to the compact types. There are spring, summer, and winter cabbages, and all are grown in the same way—they are just sown and planted at different times of year.

Basic needs
Choose a large container 8in. (20cm) or more deep. Grow bags are not deep enough. Cabbages like rich, firm soil so use equal parts soil-based potting mix, garden soil, and well-rotted organic matter.

Growing techniques
1 Before sowing, firm the potting mix in the pot down well. Sow thinly.

2 As the plants grow, pull up and firm the potting mix around each bare stem to stop it from toppling over.

3 Keep the plants from drying out and water well as their heads start to form.

4 Apply high-nitrogen fertilizer throughout the growing season.

Problem solving
Keep plants covered with netting to protect them from birds, flea beetles (see p35), and cabbage white butterflies. Look out for clusters of eggs on the undersides of leaves and pick off before they hatch into hungry caterpillars, which seem to prefer green cabbages to red types (see p35).

Expert tips

- All-purpose soilless mix is too loosely textured for growing cabbages.
- Cabbages will not head up unless they are held firmly in the potting mix.

Harvesting and storage
Gather young leaves for greens as soon as they are big enough. Otherwise wait until the cabbage head has a solid head, then cut the stem just above the potting mix. Making a cross in the remaining stump will stimulate it to resprout, giving you a second, smaller crop. Winter cabbage can be left to stand in the pot until you are ready to eat it, but cut other types before the first frosts of the fall and store in net bags. Cabbage does not freeze.

VARIETIES green: 'Pixie', 'Minicole', 'Shelta'; red: 'Redcap', 'Rodeo'

Cabbages need firm soil around their bases to keep them upright and help them form good, strong heads. Keep mounding the soil and firming around plants.

Small, compact types are great for containers—harvest young leaves or allow cabbages to form dense heads.

Kale

This great, hardy, winter vegetable is one of the easiest leafy vegetables to grow—it can cope with cold weather better than other brassicas and is finally gaining the popularity it deserves. Attractive, curly, dwarf kale works really well in pots and will provide plenty of delicious pickings throughout winter and spring.

Basic needs
Likes well-drained, nutrient-rich potting mix in a pot 8in. (20cm) or more deep.

Growing techniques
1 Sow seed thinly from midspring to midsummer in rows, or dot plants among other crops.

2 Mulch to conserve water and do not allow plants to dry out.

3 Feed young plants once to give them a boost.

4 When established, pick leaves regularly to keep young growth coming and nip off flower shoots.

Expert tips

- If planting out as young transplants, set kale right up to its first leaves in the potting mix and firm in well.
- Kale plants can tolerate a slightly shady position in the yard.

Problem solving
Net plants if birds are a problem—it is said birds prefer the green types of kale to the red ones.

Harvesting and storage
Some kale plants can be harvested as cut-and-come-again salad crops. Start picking these once the plants are 2in. (5cm) tall; more young leaves will grow. Pick other types when leaves are young and tender—initially harvest the top ones, from early fall. Once the crown has been harvested, pick new sideshoots from midwinter to late spring, until plants go to seed. Eat leaves fresh or store in a refrigerator for a few days.

VARIETIES black: 'Nero di Toscana'; green: 'Afro', 'Bornick', 'Fribor', 'Red Russian', 'Reflex', 'Starbor', 'Winterbor'; red: 'Redbor'

Kale is a must-have crop that is easy, full of flavor, and nutritious. Plant it alone or among other crops.

Kale keeps on producing leaves if picked regularly. A couple of pots should give a constant supply of fresh, tender leaves.

Lettuces & salads

Lettuces are quick, easy to grow, ridiculously productive, and bring a fantastic range of color and texture to as small or large a container as you wish to use. Although there are heading types, such as romaine, and looseleaf ones, all can be picked as cut-and-come-again plants that will continue cropping for months and make the most enticing mixed salads. And if you choose the right varieties you can grow salads year-round. Devote whole pots to salads or dot plants among other crops while waiting for them to come up.

Basic needs

Grow in any container 4in. (10cm) or more deep, including a window box, pot, trough, or grow bag. Fill with three parts all-purpose potting mix combined with one part garden compost.

Growing techniques

1 Sow spring and summer salads from early spring, in short rows every couple of weeks for a steady supply and to reduce gluts. They are good grown as cut-and-come-again plants because this minimizes their chances of bolting in hot, dry weather. For winter and early spring leaves sow seed in late summer and early fall, and cover plants with temporary row covers.

2 Place the containers of lettuces and other salad crops in full sun or a bright, well-lit site.

3 Water well in dry weather in the mornings, to prevent leaf scorch as well as attacks by slugs, which are more likely if plants are watered in the evening. Too little water can make heading lettuces bolt. Winter lettuces can be pretty much left to cope on their own provided that they are moist. All lettuces need regular feeding.

Heading lettuces are brilliant dotted anywhere you have room—among other crops or occupying the odd spare pot.

Grow rows of colorful and differently shaped, cut-and-come-again leaves for a regular supply of mixed salad.

Containers filled with mizuna, lettuce, and mustard provide tasty mixtures and are especially attractive when flowers such as forget-me-not (*Myosotis*) are added.

Problem solving

Slugs and snails adore young seedlings, so protect pots and plants particularly well at this vulnerable stage of development (see p32). Damp, cold summers may result in gray mold. Pick off infected growth when you spot it and do not plant too densely. Lettuces are prone to bolt in hot, dry weather.

Harvesting and storage

Heading lettuces are ready as soon as a firm head has formed. Cut with a sharp knife in the morning when they are fresh. Harvest cut-and-come-again leaves only when you need them; they will not stay fresh for long. Cut leaves from the base with scissors, taking a few from each plant. If you need to store them dampen with water and keep airtight in the refrigerator.

Expert tips

- Water potting mix before sowing rather than after, to ensure the seed is in contact with moist soil (see p132).

- Lettuces like sun but need cool to germinate so if sowing in the hottest months place pots in the shade, sow in the morning, and water with cool water.

- Sow seed closely for cut-and-come-again crops; set farther apart if leaving to head.

- Water regularly so the soil is moist. As soon as lettuce is stressed it bolts.

VARIETIES chicory: 'Indigo'; corn salad; heading lettuce: 'Claremont', 'Little Gem', 'Pinokkio', 'Ravel', 'Sunny', 'Winter Density'; looseleaf lettuce: 'Cocarde', 'Green Oak Leaf', 'Red Salad Bowl'

Summer-long salads

Growing your own mixed salad is simple and can be done at a fraction of the cost of the prepacked bags available at the supermarket. Sow a mixture of heading varieties and cut-and-come-again leaves into wooden boxes, such as recycled crates, and you will have a handy supply of fresh leaves that can sit anywhere, even on a windowsill.

Lettuces and other salad leaves are brilliantly undemanding crops that can be sown any time between spring and late summer. With protection from temporary row covers, crops can even be sown in the fall for picking throughout winter. Before you fill any wooden container with potting mix always line it with plastic—something like an old soil-mix bag is perfect—to stop the wood from rotting and to prevent any preservatives in the wood leaching into the soil. After germination you need to thin heading types to give them

room to develop, but don't waste the thinnings—these can be eaten too. Cut-and-come-again leaves are harvested sufficiently young that they don't need further thinning, provided that they are sown thinly in the first place. Place your crates in sun or dappled shade (see p131) and keep the potting mix moist, especially in a hot summer, because some salad crops run to seed in the blink of an eye.

Opposite: Sow a box of salad every couple of weeks for a continuous supply of fresh leaves throughout the summer.

Sowing your salad box

What you need
- recycled wooden crate or box; ■ plastic liner; ■ scissors; ■ drainage material (see p15); ■ all-purpose potting mix; ■ garden compost; ■ dibble; ■ salad seed—ready mix combinations and single varieties (see p131).

1 Line the wooden box with the plastic and cut drainage holes in the liner with scissors. Cover the base with drainage material. While filling the box with a mix of potting soil and garden compost (see p130), hold the liner tightly to each edge of the box. Water the soil.

2 Make two or three shallow furrows in the potting mix using either a wooden dibble or your finger. Take a pinch of seed and sprinkle it thinly along each furrow and then draw the potting mix over the seed with your finger and thumb.

3 When the seedlings of heading types are ³/₄in. (2cm) high thin them so that you have four or five plants per row. Water and feed lettuces regularly. Protect them from slugs and snails (see p32).

4 Harvest cut-and-come again leaves regularly once they are about 2in. (5cm) high (see p131), or let them grow to about 6in. (15cm), giving them a light thin so plants have more space. You can then cut off their entire heads.

5 Traditional heading lettuces are picked whole in one go by pulling up the whole plant or by cutting plants with a sharp knife just above the surface of the potting mix

Oriental leaves

Oriental leaves is a catch-all term for an increasingly popular group of leafy veg and salads such as bok choy, Chinese cabbage, and mizuna. All are full of punch and texture and are very useful in the kitchen. They can be grown as large heads or as cut-and-come-again baby leaves. Most Oriental leaf vegetables will provide you with fresh leaves from midsummer to early winter.

Basic needs
Most types need a pot 6in. (15cm) or more deep filled with good-quality, moisture-retentive soil. Devote a whole pot to Oriental leaves or dot plants among other crops.

Growing techniques
1 Sow thinly from midspring to midsummer in a sheltered, sunny place (see p137).

2 Keep the plants well watered and fed to prevent bolting and improve flavor. Chinese cabbage has shallow roots so water little and often.

Problem solving
Slugs love the young leaves and can reduce the

Expert tip

- Cover plants with temporary row covers in the fall to extend your harvesting period.

head of a Chinese cabbage to mush so always control them (see p32). Protect Chinese cabbage against cabbage white caterpillars and flea beetles with netting (see p35).

Harvesting and storage
Most are quick growers: pick cut-and-come-again baby leaves just a couple of weeks after germination; whole plants should be ready for harvesting after about 10 weeks. Leaves will not keep well so gather only what you need. Stumps of most whole plants will resprout giving you more young leaves for a second or third harvest. Use the leaves in salads, stir-fries, or broths.

VARIETIES bok choy: 'Canton Dwarf', 'Purple', 'Summer Breeze', 'Tah Tsai', Tatsoi'; Chinese cabbage: 'Kasumi', 'One Kilo', 'Yuki'; giant red mustard; mibuna; mizuna

Mizuna will grow and grow, no matter how much you cut it, even continuing through winter in warm-temperate areas.

The leaves of mibuna can get tough when plants bolt in hot weather. Their flavor is slightly hotter than that of mizuna.

Arugula

Punchy, peppery arugula is a simple salad crop that can also be cooked and has edible flowers. There are salad and wild types; all are easy to grow, which is great news considering how much arugula costs to buy in the stores.

Basic needs
Grow in a pot, trough, window box, or grow bag, 4in. (10cm) deep, filled with soil-based potting mix.

Growing techniques
1 Sow thinly in a slightly shaded spot, from midspring to early fall (see p155).

2 Thin seedlings to 4in. (10cm) apart.

3 As plants bolt easily, sow arugula every couple of weeks. Protect fall sowings over winter in cool-temperate climates with temporary row covers.

4 Keep arugula watered to stop plants running to seed, but do not overdo it—too much water dilutes the taste. Feed plants regularly.

5 Nip off the flower buds—they are edible too.

Problem solving
Flea beetles can get very bad, defoliating the plants (see p35). Use a fine-mesh net.

Harvesting and storage
Arugula is ready to crop in as little as four weeks from sowing. Harvest it as a cut-and-come-again crop or as whole plants. Pick often to keep growth tender. Eat leaves fresh or make into pesto.

VARIETIES 'Apollo', 'Buzz', 'Runway', 'Skyarugula', 'Sweet Oakleaf', 'Wild Grazia'

Both wild and salad varieties of arugula can be harvested as cut-and-come-again leaves or entire plants can be plucked.

Expert tip
■ Allowing some plants to set seed is a good way to extend and increase your crop.

Arugula flowers are pretty *en masse*. If you leave your last crop to self seed you will have new plants next year.

Some like it hot

Asian food is renowned for its spicy kick, which you can recreate if you fill this simple terra-cotta pot full of the flavors of the Orient. Fresh chili peppers will add a fiery punch to curries or soups, while the peppery leaves of mizuna and mibuna give a lively note to salads. Mature leaves of bok choy are excellent in Asian broths and its baby leaves for use in stir-fries. The fresh leaves of Asian greens look lovely against terra-cotta, and they work just as well in a plastic window box near the kitchen to keep everything handy.

Chili peppers take a long time to grow and ripen over the summer. The hotter the temperatures the quicker they will mature (see p83), but if the weather is poor it can take until the fall before peppers are ripe. To give yourself a headstart you might prefer to buy chili peppers as young plants from the garden center or by mail order and plant them out directly into the final pot when frosts have passed. Set them in your warmest, sunniest spot. Pinch back the growing tips after planting to encourage bushy growth and give your plant liquid 5–5–10 fertilizer every week after the flowers appear. To enhance your crop, you can pollinate the flowers yourself (see p86). Depending on variety, plants may need staking as they grow to avoid them becoming top-heavy with fruit and the branches snapping.

Mizuna and mibuna are two of the easiest and most rewarding crops you can grow (see p134). As long as they are picked regularly and any flowering growth is nipped off before they bolt they will go on and on producing fresh, tangy leaves. Bok choy however is particularly prone to bolting, especially in times of stress, usually drought, so ensure the pot is kept well watered. If you are worried about premature bolting, try specially selected seed that has been chosen for strong growth (which includes bolt resistance), good germination rates, and pest and disease resistance. It is more expensive than ordinary seed but is much more likely to succeed. Each seed should germinate so there is no need to oversow to ensure you have enough plants.

Harvest mibuna and mizuna leaves whenever you need them—they start to deteriorate quickly after picking. Both plants should grow strongly, and in milder areas will carry on right through the winter.

Planting your Asian greens

What you need

- terra-cotta pot 12in. (30cm) in diameter;
- drainage material (see p15);
- all-purpose potting mix;
- chili pepper plant;
- mibuna, mizuna, and bok choy seed.

1 Line the bottom of the pot with drainage material and fill it with potting mix until it is three quarters full. Plant the chili pepper in the center of the pot at the same level it was in its previous pot and fill in with more potting mix. Water well.

2 Make a shallow furrow along each edge of the pot with your finger and sow two sides with mibuna seed and one side with mizuna seed, covering the seed as you go.

3 Sow bok choy seed on the fourth side. Cover it with potting mix so that it is at the depth recommended on the seed packet.

4 Water the seed in well to help establishment and germination. Then keep the potting mix moist—never let it dry out. Feed the plants regularly. Protect the young plants against slugs and snails (see p32).

5 Thin the seedlings to allow individual plants to grow strongly. Bok choy needs more room than mizuna and mibuna, which can be used as cut-and-come-again leaves (see p134). Eat the thinnings in salads. Harvest the first chili peppers when they are green (see p87).

Herbs

Both the flowers and slender, tubular leaves of chives are edible, adding a tangy, onion punch to any meal.

Chives

Chives (*Allium schoenoprasum*), with their fresh, onion bite, are indispensable in the kitchen, easy to grow, and very happy in pots. Their neat, edible, pom-pom flowers are loved by bees and other pollinators (see p24).

Basic needs
Given a minimum depth of 4in. (10cm), chives will thrive in containers, hanging baskets, and window boxes. Use soil-based potting mix because chives prefer rich, moist to well-drained soil.

Growing techniques
■ Sow seed in early spring, placing the pot on a sunny windowsill at 68°F (20°C); transplant outside once there is little risk of frosts. Alternatively sow directly outside from late spring to early summer.

Bees and other pollinating insects buzz merrily around chives' flowers in summer.

■ Chives cope with sun and partial shade.

■ Mulch in spring and nip off flowerheads before they fade to encourage leaf growth.

■ Every 2–3 years divide clumps in spring (see p105) or replace plants.

Problem solving
Overcrowding can make plants susceptible to rust, which causes bright yellow spots on the leaves. Cut infected plants back right away.

Harvesting and storage
Chives can be harvested once they are 6in. (15cm) high by cutting leaves 1¼in. (3cm) from the base. Continue harvesting until first frosts.

VARIETIES 'Corsican White', 'Pink Perfection'; *A. tuberosum*

Dill

Feathery foliage and sprays of yellow flowers make dill (*Anethum graveolens*) a very pretty centerpiece in a mixed herb pot. Its fresh, mild leaves and sharper seeds are outstanding in soups and salads. Dill flowers attract beneficial insects. Do not grow near fennel as these plants cross-pollinate and their offspring will have diluted flavors.

Basic needs
Fill any pot of 12in. (30cm) diameter or more with all-purpose potting mix combined with grit.

Growing techniques
■ Sow seed directly into pots outside after the frosts, or plant out young plants.

■ Grow in a sheltered spot with a little shade.

■ Keep picking for fresh growth and compact, bushy plants. Never cut dill right back.

■ Dill is short-lived and bolts if even slightly dry, so grow successively for a constant supply.

■ Stake whole plants if necessary, using peasticks and twine.

Allow dill to run to flower at the end of the season and then pick the seedheads for drying just as they ripen.

Problem solving

Slugs and snails adore dill so take protective measures around your container and plants to keep these pests away (see p34).

Harvesting and storage

Leaves can be picked about two months after sowing. Eat them fresh, store in the refrigerator for a couple of weeks, or freeze leaves, chopped and mixed with water, in ice-cube trays. Once seed starts to ripen pop stems in a paper bag to dry. They will all ripen at the same time, so be quick off the mark. Store in an airtight container.

VARIETIES 'Diana', 'Herkules', 'Tetra'

Horseradish

Horseradish (*Armoracia rusticana*) is much better when grown in a pot, because it is invasive and tenacious in open soil. It is an easy, unfussy, hardy perennial that will provide you with a regular supply of fresh, peppery roots that you are very unlikely to find in the stores. It will last for several years.

Harvest the roots of horseradish by lifting plants in the fall. Use what you need and store the rest in damp sand before planting them again in spring.

Basic needs

Use a large, deep tub, pot, or old garbage can. Fill with soil-based potting mix that has been combined with grit, for drainage.

Growing techniques

■ Sow seed; or root cuttings (thongs), 6in. (15cm) long, in dibbled holes in potting mix. The cutting will grow whichever way up you plant it.

■ Horseradish likes a sunny site, but tolerates a little shade.

■ Water in dry periods and feed with seaweed fertilizer during summer.

Problem solving

Cover with netting to stop cabbage white caterpillars munching on the leaves (see p35).

Harvesting and storage

Young leaves can be picked for use fresh or dried, and roots can be divided or dug up when needed. Alternatively lift the whole plant for harvest in the fall and store the roots in boxes of sand for use later or for planting again as thongs in spring to create new plants. Roots can be grated or sliced when fresh or be stored in vinegar. They also keep in the refrigerator for up to a week. Horseradish loses its flavor completely if cooked.

VARIETIES 'Variegata'

Cilantro

This distinctive, pungent annual has gorgeous leaves and wonderful seeds—even the flowers and roots are edible. Cilantro (*Coriandrum sativum*) is easily grown from seed and is a bargain in terms of cropping potential.

Basic needs
Use a well-drained pot, 4in. (10cm) deep, filled with all-purpose potting mix.

Growing techniques
■ Sow seed from spring onward. Wait until there is little risk of frosts if you wish to sow outside (see p144).

■ Choose a warm but shaded spot (see p144) if growing for leaves; seeds ripen best in full sun.

■ Sow successional pots, every 3–4 weeks.

■ Keep plants well watered because cilantro bolts at the slightest upset. Liquid feed every two weeks through the growing season.

Problem solving
Tends to be trouble-free.

Harvesting and storage
Cropping can begin as soon as leaves are large enough—generally 7–9 weeks after sowing. Use leaves fresh or freeze them in ice-cube trays. In the fall cut the seedheads when they are almost ripe and put in paper bags to dry; then store the seed in airtight containers.

VARIETIES 'Calypso', 'Confetti', 'Leisure', 'Lemon', 'Morocco'

Lemongrass

This increasingly popular herb is often used in Asian cuisine for its sweet, lemony scent. The striking canes of lemongrass (*Cymbopogon citratus*) look graceful in pots.

Basic needs
Needs a large pot at least 16in. (40cm) wide. Add grit to garden compost or soil-based potting mix.

Growing techniques
■ Grow lemongrass outside only where night temperatures do not fall below 55°F (13°C); otherwise cultivate them indoors.

■ Grow from young plants or by rooting a stem in a glass of water then planting it up. Sow seed at 68°F (20°C); it takes 2–3 weeks to germinate.

■ Do not let plants dry out in summer, and give a weekly liquid feed through the growing season.

■ Plants will go dormant once temperatures and light levels start to drop, so reduce watering and cut leaves back to 4in. (10cm) above the stems.

■ Protect lemongrass from frost over winter.

■ Divide plants by gently teasing apart with your fingers. Pot up right away into a container that fits snugly round the roots—lemongrass loves to be rootbound.

Problem solving
Keep plants practically dry and frost-free in winter since they are prone to mildew (see p34) and rot.

Cilantro is quick to run to seed so grow pots of it successionally or sow it at intervals dotted among other crops for a continuous supply.

Lemongrass is ideal in a container in cool-temperate climates, so it can be moved indoors for protection over winter.

All parts of this aniseed-flavored plant are edible, including the seeds, which can be eaten both fresh and dried.

Harvesting and storage

Both leaves and stems can be harvested throughout the growing season to be used fresh or dried. Cut the stems at soil level and use the bottom 4in. (10cm) of each stem.

VARIETIES Only the species is grown.

Fennel

Closely related to the bulbous fennel, this feathery fennel (*Foeniculum vulgare*) is grown for its perky, aniseed leaves, seeds, and even its flowers. When dotted through a large, mixed container, this airy plant makes a stunning feature. Colored foliage varieties are particularly attractive.

Basic needs

Plant in any pot, tub, or window box, 12in. (30cm) deep, that has plenty of drainage holes. Give fennel well-drained, moisture-retentive potting mix, with some grit added in. Never grow fennel too near dill or cilantro—they cross-pollinate, and their offspring have less flavor.

Growing techniques

■ Purchase young plants, or sow seed directly outside, from midspring to early summer.

■ Give fennel a sunny spot.

■ Water regularly and mulch around plants with garden compost. This will stop the fennel plants going to seed too quickly.

■ For a supply of fresh, young leaves remove the flowerheads at once and shorten stems to 12in. (30cm) above ground level in midsummer.

■ Remove old stems after plants have died back.

Problem solving

Keep an eye out for slugs, which love the young shoots. Hide beer traps in pots (see p32).

Harvesting and storage

Everything is edible. Pick the leaves, young stems, and unripe seeds to use fresh when you need them. Ripe seeds can be dried and stored for use later. Leaves can be frozen as well as infused in oil or vinegar as a flavoring.

VARIETIES 'Purpureum', 'Rubrum'

Cilantro in a colander

Cilantro is a fast, easy crop that lasts only a few weeks, so sow a fresh pot every month for a constant supply throughout summer. Fortunately the entire plant is edible, and the delicious, fragrant seeds can be added to curries and casseroles. A recycled colander is an ideal container for crops that love free-draining soil.

Cilantro is best sown directly where it is to be grown, rather than in a smaller pot and potted up, since it hates having its roots disturbed. Wait until all frosts have passed and then sow seed into free-draining potting mix. An all-purpose one is fine for a short-term crop such as this. Place the container where it will be in shade for some of the day—plants will quickly bolt if in full sunlight all day—but they do need warmth. Cilantro is best sown little and often, because it bolts readily when the soil dries out (see p142), and this way

you will not waste your crop. Keep sowing fresh supplies until late summer. Plants should be ready to crop 7–9 weeks after sowing. Pick regularly to encourage fresh, young leaves and healthy, compact plants; such harvesting methods will also stop cilantro from flowering. Cilantro hates damp soil so water it in the morning rather than at night.

Opposite: Cilantro is a lush, bright crop that imparts its distinctive fragrance and lemony flavor to Asian and Indian cooking and is also delicious in salads and sandwiches.

Planting your cilantro

What you need
- hanging basket liner;
- aluminum colander or any pot 4in. (10cm) or more deep with good drainage; ■ scissors;
- square of plastic from an old soil-mix bag; ■ all-purpose potting mix; ■ cilantro seed.

1 Place the liner in the colander. You may need to trim around the edge and overlap the liner inside to get it to fit. Lay a square of plastic in the center to help retain some moisture.

2 Fill the colander with potting soil and firm it down gently with your fingers until the potting soil is about 2in. (5cm) below the rim. Leaving this gap at the top will make watering easier.

3 Space the cilantro seed evenly over the potting soil. Then gently push them just into the potting soil surface.

4 Sprinkle potting soil over the seed, sifting it through your fingers to give a light dusting. Water well and place the colander in a warm spot in the yard with partial shade during some of the day. Keep the potting soil moist at all times.

5 Feed plants regularly (see p142). Pick cilantro leaves often. When plants start to go to seed, you can either dispose of the plant or allow the seed to develop until it's almost ripe, then cut off the entire seedhead and hang it somewhere warm to dry.

Herbal window box

Fresh herbs are bursting with flavor and packed full of vitamins and essential oils. They are expensive to buy but very easy to grow yourself, so a simple window box full of herbs is a must-have. Add the smiling faces of some edible pansy flowers to your display and you have an extra-colorful dimension you just won't find in the stores. Keep the window box close to the kitchen so you can snip off fresh leaves whenever you need them.

All of these plants can be grown from seed. Parsley is notoriously erratic and slow to germinate (see p153). Both fennel (see p143) and parsley hate being moved, so for best results buy small plants from the garden center once the weather has warmed up in late spring. Parsley is a biennial, so you'll need to buy a fresh supply for your pots every year, but if grown in a sheltered spot it should give you fresh leaves almost year-round. Fennel is an airy, aromatic perennial, grown for its warm, aniseed-flavored leaves, seeds, and flowers. Fennel may need staking to keep it looking good and should be repotted every year. Pansies are undemanding, edible flowers that grow well in loose, rich soil and have a sweet, grassy tang.

Opposite: Place the window box in a warm, sheltered spot with some light shade to stop your parsley bolting. Warmth will help to generate the essential oils that give herbs their distinctive flavor and aroma.

Planting your herbal window box

What you need
- window box, at least 24 x 8in. (60 x 20cm), that fits comfortably and is level on your windowsill;
- drainage material such as pieces of broken terra-cotta pieces, pebbles, or gravel (see p15);
- soil-based potting mix and grit, mixed 2:1;
- 2 x parsley (*Petroselinum crispum*), 2 x fennel (*Foeniculum vulgare*), 2 x pansies (*Viola x wittrockiana*).

1 Drainage is important for herbs so punch holes in the base of your window box if necessary. Then line the bottom of the box with a generous layer of drainage material.

2 Half fill the box with potting mix. Then, while they are still in their pots, arrange the plants in your window box until you are happy with the way they look. Alternating the herbs and then dotting the pansies in-between works well.

3 Remove each plant in turn from its pot, starting with the tall fennel. Gently tease out its roots to help them spread out and establish quickly when replanted. Then plant the parsley and finally insert the pansies among the herbs.

4 Top up the box with potting soil. Water well and mulch, then place the box on the windowsill. During the growing season water the plants and feed them every week with an all-purpose liquid fertilizer. Pick the leaves and flowers little and often, to promote growth.

Hyssop is the perfect choice for a pot on a deck, where its lovely scent can be enjoyed on warm, sunny days.

Hyssop

It can be difficult to buy hyssop (*Hyssopus officinalis*), so grow your own supply of this classic Mediterranean herb. The whole plant is deliciously aromatic, especially on hot summer evenings. Its vivid blue, white, or pink flowers attract butterflies and bees.

Basic needs

Grow in any pot, of 12in. (30cm) diameter or more, with plenty of drainage holes. Prefers light, well-drained potting mix combined with grit.

Growing techniques

■ Sow directly into sun-warmed soil in late spring or buy young plants.

■ Loves a sunny spot against a south-facing wall.

■ Trim the plants back in spring. Feed regularly with comfrey fertilizer once flowers appear, and deadhead promptly to keep hyssop flowering.

■ Protect plants in winter with temporary row covers if temperatures fall below 23°F (-5°C).

■ Replace plants every four years.

Problem solving

Tends to be trouble-free.

Harvesting and storage

Pick leaves from the top to encourage bushy growth. Use fresh, dried, or preserve in olive oil. Harvest flowers just as they open; they are lovely in salads or drinks.

VARIETIES f. *albus*, subsp. *aristatus*, 'Roseus'

Bay

The dark green, evergreen leaves of bay (*Laurus nobilis*) are an essential ingredient in a bouquet garni, so keep this plant by the kitchen door for easy pickings.

Basic needs

Grow in any container, 12in. (30cm) or more deep, filled with rich, gritty, soil-based potting mix for good drainage and stability.

Growing techniques

■ Buy young plants, because seed germination is erratic and cuttings can be difficult to propagate.

■ Plant between midspring and early fall in a bright, sheltered spot. Water plants well.

■ Give a liquid feed every couple of weeks from midspring to late summer. Water sparingly, particularly in winter—raising the pot on bricks helps water drain away easily.

■ If temperatures drop below 41°F (5°C) protect bay plants with temporary row cover.

■ Repot every two years.

Problem solving

Yellow leaves could be caused by a nutrient deficiency, waterlogged potting mix,

The fresh leaves of bay are one of the herbs in a bouquet garni, for use in casseroles, sauces, and soups. The other popular ingredients are oregano, basil, and thyme.

Pot-grown bays can be kept in check by trimming with pruners into cones, pyramids, or standards.

or harsh weather. Scale insects cause an ugly, sooty mold; wipe off by hand or wash with insecticidal soap. Bay suckers distort and thicken leaves; cut back affected branches.

Harvesting and storage

Pick the foliage year-round. Fresh leaves have a stronger flavor than dried. Bay leaves dry well and can also be preserved in vinegar.

VARIETIES 'Aurea', f. *angustifolia*

Mint

Another tenacious yard invader, mint (*Mentha*) is much better grown in containers. This essential kitchen herb has different scents, flavors, and leaf shapes, most of which are unavailable in the stores.

Basic needs

Needs a minimum container depth of 6in. (15cm) and rich, gritty potting mix (see p14).

Growing techniques

■ Grow from young plants, or root cuttings from established ones by digging up a piece of root in

the growing season, and cutting by a green node. Place in a pot of seed starter mix. Water well.

■ Give plants semishade, or a sunnier spot if growing a colored-leaf type.

■ Ensure different mints are not grown close by, or they hybridize and their offspring lose flavor.

■ Liquid feed regularly during the growing season and do not let the potting mix dry out.

■ Deadhead regularly. Tidy up plants in summer.

■ Divide plants every three years.

Problem solving

If you see the brown leaf spots of mint rust, destroy the plant; do not replant in the same pot.

Harvesting and storage

Use fresh leaves throughout the growing season or freeze, rather than dry them.

VARIETIES *M.* x gracilis 'Variegata', *M.* x *smithiana*, *M. spicata*, *M. s.* var. *crispa* 'Moroccan', *M. s.* 'Tashkent', *M. suaveolens*, *M. s.* 'Variegata', *M.* x *villosa* var. *alopecuroides*

Mentha suaveolens 'Variegata' (top left) is slow growing and perfect for use in a pot. The leaves of *M.* x *gracilis* 'Variegata' (above left) have a warm, gentle flavor, while *M. spicata* (above right) is the best mint for sauces and jellies.

Mint medley

Thanks to their thuggish tendencies mints are often thought of as the baddies of the herb world, but a neat trick is to grow them in pots to stop them rampaging over other plants. This applies even when growing with other mints. To enjoy a range of their pungent leaves grow different mints (see p149) in separate pots inside a single, large pot or other planter. Mint is a shallow-rooting plant, so there is no point in planting it in a very deep pot.

Plant this seasonal project in spring, using light, gritty potting mix, both in the pots and within the larger planter. Before plunging the individual pots into the final planter, pot each mint plant on into a larger container to allow it a little room to spread. The mint roots will soon grow through the bottom of their pot into the potting soil below. Place the planter in partial shade—you don't want this leafy crop to dry out too quickly. Feed plants regularly (see p149).

By growing mints closely together there is a risk they may hybridize if the plants are allowed to flower and set seed, and their resulting seed and seedlings will have diluted flavors and scents. To prevent this trim and harvest the leaves regularly. This keeps the plants bushy and compact, and there will be no flowers.

Opposite: Harvest mint by nipping off the stems near the growing tips with your fingers or cutting them off with scissors. Regular nipping will prevent undesirable flowering.

Planting your mint medley

What you need

- all-purpose potting mix;
- horticultural grit;
- shallow container or trough such as this verdigris planter;
- 3 or 4 different mint plants (see p149) such as apple mint (*M. suaveolens*), pineapple mint (*M. s.* 'Variegata'), red mint (*M. x smithiana*), and Tashkent mint (*M. spicata* 'Tashkent');
- pots for potting up individual mint plants;
- decorative gravel for topdressing.

1 Mix the potting mix together with a little grit in a ratio of two parts potting soil to one part grit. Pot up all the mints into pots a size larger than the ones they originally came in. Water each well.

2 Half fill the planter with the potting soil, leaving enough room for the mints to sit on it in their pots, as well as space at the top to make it easy when watering.

3 Sit your mint pots on the potting soil in the planter. Make sure the tops of all the pots are level and fill in the gaps with more potting soil until it is up to the soil level in each mint pot. Water in well.

4 Topdress with gravel to keep moisture away from the crowns of the plants and to hold moisture in the soil. Water and feed the plants regularly to encourage growth.

Common or sweet basil (top right) is the popular choice for pesto and pasta sauces. Despite Greek basil (above left) having the smallest leaves of all it still has a strong flavor. Red basil (above right) has lovely, pungent, purple leaves.

Basil

This popular supermarket herb is so much better when homegrown. Basil (*Ocimum basilicum*) is a perfect match in the kitchen as well as in the yard (see p27).

Basic needs
Sow seed directly into pots after the frosts, or into individual pots or cell packs indoors filled with all-purpose soilless mix combined with grit.

Growing techniques
■ Sow from late winter to midspring. Seed is light sensitive so press it gently into the potting mix and do not cover. Water well.

■ Seed germinates quicker on a warm, sunny windowsill, at 68–77°F (20–25°C). Once germinated set pots in a sunny, sheltered spot.

■ In cool-temperate areas grow basil under glass or indoors on a windowsill.

■ Basil hates to sit in water overnight, so water only in the morning; the plant can then use up the water before nightfall.

Problem solving
Spray plants with water or insecticidal soap if they are attacked by greenfly or whitefly (see p34).

Harvesting and storage
Pick young leaves regularly from the tips (see p155). Store in the refrigerator for a few days or freeze individual leaves, make into pesto, or infuse in oil or vinegar. Use the aromatic flowers in salads.

VARIETIES 'Cinnamon', 'Horapha', 'Napolitano', 'Nufar', 'Purple Ruffles', 'Sweet Genovase'

Oregano

Oregano (*Origanum vulgare*) is grown for its sweet, pungent leaves, which have a more intense flavor than those of its delicate sibling, marjoram. Some varieties make nice features in their own pot, while low-growing, creeping types such as 'Nanum' are perfect for edging larger pots. The beautiful, aromatic flowers attract butterflies.

Basic needs
Requires a pot 12in. (30cm) or more deep and rich soil-based potting mix or garden compost combined with horticultural grit for drainage.

Growing techniques
■ Propagate from cuttings of young growth in spring, or buy young plants. Oregano does not grow readily from seed.

■ Plant in a sunny spot. Water well after planting and then regularly during dry weather.

■ Trim plants after flowering to stop them becoming straggly.

■ Cut down within 2¼in. (6cm) of the soil before plants die back in winter. Mulch with grit to protect the crowns from winter wet. Protect plants from hard frosts.

Oregano leaves can be picked and used fresh, dried, or even frozen long after the plant has died down for winter.

Problem solving
Tends to be trouble-free.

Harvesting and storage
Pick bunches of leaves just before the flowers open and dry by hanging them somewhere warm and airy. Oregano leaves can also be infused in fragrant oils or vinegars.

VARIETIES 'Aureum', 'Compactum', 'Nanum'

Parsley

As it is one of the most versatile and common kitchen herbs, parsley (*Petroselinum crispum*) is an essential in window boxes or in handy pots by the kitchen door. It is generally grown as an annual because plants go to seed in their second year and so lose their usefulness as a cutting herb. Choose from the many varieties of flat-leaved or curly-leaved parsley.

Basic needs
Grow in any container, including a hanging basket, with a depth of 8in. (20cm) or more. Do not bother with the "parsley pots" sold in garden

Curly-leaved parsley has a milder flavor than flat-leaved parsley. For the best flavor add parsley just before the end of cooking.

centers. They are tricky to water and too small for parsley's large taproot. This herb is a hungry plant, so add garden compost or other organic matter to its potting mix.

Growing techniques
■ Sow outside in late spring, only just covering the seed. Parsley is slow and sometimes erratic to germinate, although a warm spot, damp soil, and covering with temporary row cover will help.

■ Prefers damp shade so do not let plants dry out.

■ Nip off flowerheads to encourage further leaf growth during the growing season.

■ Cover plants with temporary row cover again in the fall to slow down winter dieback.

Problem solving
Slugs love young parsley plants so protect plants with grit or crushed shells (see p32).

Harvesting and storage
Pick fresh leaves whenever you need them. They can be frozen in sealed polyethylene bags or chopped and frozen in water in ice-cube trays.

VARIETIES curly-leaved: 'Champion Moss Curled'; flat-leaved: 'Italian Giant'

Taste of Italy

Italian food is all about top-quality ingredients and distinctive flavors and where better to get the best than from your own homegrown produce. This beautifully decorated, imitation-lead pot contains the classic Mediterranean ingredients of sweet peppers, spicy arugula, and peppery basil, bringing a taste of Italy to the yard as well as the plate.

Unless you start sowing seed very early in spring, it is best to buy young sweet pepper plants from the garden center or by mail order since they need a long, hot summer in which to grow, flower, and ripen (see p83). This gives you the best chance of a crop. Basil seed can be sown from early spring onward and the timing is nowhere near as critical, but if time or space is short these can also be bought as young plants and planted out (see p152). The arugula can be sown all at once or a section at a time. It is very quick to bolt if conditions are not exactly right (see p135), and this way you can sow a section every couple of weeks and always have a new harvest coming up as another goes over.

Plant up this Mediterranean pot once all frosts have passed, sowing the arugula in the gaps in-between the peppers and basil. Make sure the pot is in a sunny position to help warm and ripen the fruit. Pinching back the basil tips will encourage bushier growth and more young leaves to develop; it will also deter plants from bolting so soon. Feed the peppers with a liquid 5–5–10 fertilizer every week, once flowers appear.

Above: Most peppers will go from green to red and can be picked at whichever stage of ripening you prefer. Harvesting the first few peppers when they are still green will encourage more fruit, which can then be left to ripen further.

Left: Harvest young leaves of arugula regularly as cut-and-come-again salad leaves. Alternatively you could wait to harvest entire plants and resow for a new crop.

Planting your Italian pot

What you need

- imitation-lead pot 24in. (60cm) or more in diameter;
- drainage material (see p15);
- all-purpose potting mix;
- 2 x sweet pepper plants;
- 6–8 x basil plants;
- arugula seed;
- horticultural sand for sowing.

1 Line the base of the pot with drainage material and fill almost to the top with potting mix. Firm the potting soil down well with your fingers.

2 Set out the young plants, still in their pots, with the sweet peppers in the center and the basil plants around the edge. Ensure each plant is evenly spaced and there is enough room for the arugula to be sown in-between them. When you are happy, plant and water in the peppers and basil.

3 As arugula seed is tiny it is helpful to mix it with sand before sowing, making it easier to see that you are sowing the seed evenly.

4 Scatter the seed and sand mixture across the surface of the potting soil and then cover it lightly with a sprinkling of more potting soil. Water all the plants and seed in well. Feed and water plants regularly.

5 While the basil plants are still young pinch back the growing tips to promote bushy growth. Keep picking the leaves for healthy, compact plants. Harvest the basil (see p152), arugula (see p135), and peppers (see p83) as needed.

Rosemary

Rosemary (*Rosmarinus officinalis*) is one of the most useful culinary herbs, with a heady flavor that goes well with almost any food. It makes a striking centerpiece to a mixed herb pot, and its pale blue, sometimes white or pink flowers will attract bees to your yard.

Basic needs
Grow in a large pot, 8in. (20cm) or more deep, filled with well-drained, gritty potting mix.

Growing techniques
■ Rosemary is more reliably grown from cuttings than seed. Take cuttings from new growth in spring and plant into seed starter mix. Alternatively buy and plant out young plants. Water well.

■ Favors a sunny, sheltered spot, although rosemary copes with some shade. Young plants are vulnerable in low temperatures.

■ Pinch back tips regularly to keep plants bushy.

■ Feed and prune after flowering. Rosemary does not grow back from bare wood so do not cut it too hard; nor should you prune in the fall, when plants are susceptible to frost.

■ Replace plants in pots every five years.

Problem solving
Rosemary beetle and its larvae feed on leaves. Shake plants and catch on paper below, then trash the paper and insects (see p35). Leafhoppers can cause mottling on

You can pick the pungent leaves of this evergreen herb year-round for use in all sorts of dishes, from stews and roast meats to cordials and oils.

leaves but this is mainly a cosmetic problem, as is spittlebugs' distinctive froth on leaves.

Harvesting and storage
The leaves can be picked year-round but are a bit tougher in winter. Rosemary leaves dry well; they can also be frozen and infused in oils and vinegar.

VARIETIES 'Albiflorus', 'Majorca Pink', 'Miss Jessopp's Upright', 'Prostratus'

Sage

Sage (*Salvia officinalis*) comes from a large family of annuals, perennials, and biennials, all with strongly scented, sometimes colored leaves, and heads of colorful flowers.

Basic needs
Use a large pot, 8in. (20cm) or more deep, with plenty of drainage holes. Sage needs very free-draining potting mix so add in lots of grit.

Growing techniques
■ Grow from young plants for instant harvesting or sow seed in spring. Be prepared for a wait—sage is very slow to germinate.

■ Prefers a warm, sheltered, sunny spot, although sage tolerates some shade.

■ Keep plants compact and bushy by trimming stems regularly to tame sage's woody, straggly habit. Cut back plants in spring.

■ Protect less hardy, fruit-scented *S. elegans* in cool-temperate areas throughout winter.

■ Plants will last only a few years, especially in pots, so replace old, tired plants by taking cuttings of fresh, young tips.

Problem solving
Rosemary beetles and their larvae can be a problem feeding on the leaves and flowers. Pick them off by hand or shake them off onto paper; then trash it (see p35). Leafhoppers also cause a fine, yellow mottling on leaves, but this should

Common sage, with its distinctive soft, glaucous green leaves, is best kept compact in a pot by regular picking or trimming of the leaves.

be only cosmetic damage to sage.

Harvesting and storage

Pick the evergreen leaves year-round for use with meat, particularly pork. Sage is especially good with butternut squash. Leaves are best used when fresh because they are surprisingly difficult to dry well. However when dried the flavor is extra strong so use sparingly. Remove any developing flowers.

VARIETIES 'Purpurascens', 'Tricolor'; *S. lavandulifolia*

Thyme

Low-growing, fragrant thyme (*Thymus*) could not be simpler to grow, and once planted it can be almost ignored. Some of the prettier varieties of thyme, with their variegated or colored leaves, are striking in mixed pots, particularly as edging plants or to fill in gaps, while the lovely flowers are adored by bees as they seek pollen.

Basic needs

Any pot, hanging basket, or window box with a minimum depth of 6in. (15cm) is suitable. Fill it with well-drained potting mix.

Growing techniques

■ Buy young plants or split rooted clumps from established plants and grow them on.

There is a huge range of thymes and all are suitable for growing in pots, either as colorful edging plants or taking center stage.

■ Plant in a warm, sunny spot, then water. Thereafter keep containers on the dry side; water only if there is an extended drought.

■ Pick leaves regularly to keep plants in shape.

■ Mulch pots with gravel every year to protect the crown of the plant from waterlogging.

■ Cover more tender varieties in winter to protect them from cold winds, frost, and winter wet, or move the pots to shelter.

Problem solving

Tends to be trouble-free.

Harvesting and storage

As long as you do not overharvest you can pick year-round. Thyme can be dried, frozen, or preserved in vinegar and oil. Its leaves make a great addition to stews, sauces, and marinades.

VARIETIES *T. citriodorus*, *T. pulegioides*, *T.* 'Silver Queen'

Herbal bathtub

A mixed herb pot, bursting with scent and an array of different foliage, is an attractive way to grow these useful plants, especially if they are complemented by a recycled container such as an old tin bathtub in soft, muted tones. You can enjoy fresh leaves whenever you want them—in salads, teas, even the bathtub—and at a fraction of the cost of the tiny bags available from the supermarket.

Most perennial herbs love a sunny spot and free-draining soil, so mix in plenty of grit or horticultural sand before planting. Feed plants regularly with an all-purpose liquid fertilizer, but do not be tempted to do it too often—if the leaves get too lush they lose flavor and aroma. Give the plants a trim in spring to encourage a new flush of leaves, and pick them regularly to keep them in shape. However you should never pick more than a third of the foliage at any one time, to keep plants growing strongly. To focus each plant's energies on leaf production deadhead the flowers, unless you wish to use them in salads.

Although the plants are all hardy, move the pot near the shelter of a warm wall over winter in cool-temperate areas and surround the planter in bubble wrap, making sure water can drain freely—the damp will kill the herbs, especially in cold weather. All these herbs need regular watering and feeding as well as repotting every three or four years, before they begin to get tired.

Above: Place the bathtub in a sunny, sheltered space out of cold winds and keep an eye on watering in very hot weather.

Left: Harvest leaves evenly from the tips of each plant to keep your herbs in good shape.

Planting your herbal bathtub

What you need

■ tin bathtub; ■ drill; ■ duct tape; ■ bubble wrap; ■ grit; ■ soil-based potting mix; ■ herbs such as sage, chives, thyme, rosemary, and oregano (see pp140–57); ■ gravel.

1 Drill holes through duct tape in the base of the tin bathtub—the duct tape stops the drill from slipping. Then line the sides with bubble wrap to protect it from extreme heat and cold. Add a layer of grit, to help water drain freely.

2 Add a mixture of equal parts potting mix and grit to help drainage further, filling the bathtub so that it is about two thirds full.

3 While they are still in their pots arrange the herbs in the bathtub until you are happy with the way they look together.

4 Remove the pot from each herb and plant up, filling in with potting soil until all the plants are firmly in place. Water in well.

5 Topdress with gravel to keep moisture away from the crowns of the plants. Water and feed them regularly. Trim the herbs regularly when they are in growth to keep them neat.

Edible Flowers

Allow a few self-sown borage plants to flourish around the yard to help attract pollinators each year.

Pot marigold flowers can be dried in a cooling oven and stored in jars for use long after summer has gone.

Warning: Some people have allergic reactions to unusual compounds in plants, so it is important to be cautious when trying flowers or unusual or new plants for the first time. On the first occasion, taste only a small piece (don't swallow) and have someone with you. Wait at least an hour before trying more, and then take small amounts, tasting before swallowing. If it tastes bitter, too spicy, weird, or unpalatable, don't swallow it. Spit it out. An indication that the plant might cause a reaction is a swelling or other reaction in the mouth or on the lips on first tasting.

Borage

The vivid blue flowers of borage (*Borago officinalis*) are a long-favored, edible delicacy. They have a cool, fresh, delicious, cucumber flavor, which enhances drinks and salads, and they freeze well in ice cubes. Bees and other pollinators also love these flowers (see p24). Try growing borage in a half-barrel with other such as pot marigolds (see right) and cornflowers (see opposite), or on their own, in a pot 8in. (20cm) or more deep. Borage self seeds freely.

Basic needs
Sow seed in spring and summer in a sunny spot. Borage germinates quickly, so you should be able to start picking within five weeks. Keep on picking to ensure your plants produce more.

Harvesting and storage
For flowers at their peak, harvest in the morning and use them fresh, dried, or frozen.

Pot marigold

The petals of pot marigold (*Calendula*) bring a bright orange zing and peppery spice to salads, rice, soups, and casseroles.

Basic needs
Easy-to-grow pot marigolds self seed readily. They are happy in pots (see p164), as well as window boxes, and are not fussy about potting mix or site, although you will get more flowers if you grow them in sun. Sow in spring and protect seedlings against slugs. Keep plants compact by pinching back their tips. Pick flowers regularly to ensure you have a constant supply. Wash off blackfly with insecticidal soap.

The charming, blue annual cornflower can be sown in the fall for larger, earlier flowering plants.

The beautiful heads of sunflowers follow the sun through the course of the day.

Harvesting and storage

Harvest flowers just as they are opening for use fresh or dried.

Cornflower

Curiously the electric blue flowers of cornflower (*Centaurea cyanus*) have little fragrance, yet they impart a sweet, spicy, clove flavor when eaten.

Basic needs

In an open, sunny place sow seed in the fall or late spring in large pots filled with gritty, soil-based potting mix. Be patient—cornflowers can take up to three weeks to germinate. Keep the potting mix moist until plants establish, then slow watering down. Prevent the tall, wiry stems from flopping by discreetly wrapping bunches with thread, and prolong the flowering season by regularly harvesting and deadheading. The flowers are a target for butterflies and bees so dot the plants through your pots—'Dwarf Blue Midget' is particularly successful used in this way.

Harvesting and storage

Pick flowers before they are fully open and use fresh or dried. Dry cornflowers promptly after harvesting by hanging them in a dark, airy place.

Sunflower

All floral parts of these vibrantly colored plants are edible. Sunflower (*Helianthus*) petals have a slightly nutty taste, while the tender, green buds are eaten like artichoke hearts.

Basic needs

Sow seed outside from midspring into potting mix combined with grit for extra drainage. Choose a warm, sunny spot. Cover pots with netting, and protect young plants from slugs and snails (see p32). Taller varieties may need staking.

Harvesting and storage

For buds, gather the flowers before they open. For petals, pick only the newest flowers (see p165), and for seed let the disk on the back of the flowerhead turn yellow, cut it off, and put in a paper bag. Leave until the disk is dark brown. Then eat the seeds or roast them to store in an airtight jar. Alternatively leave the seeds to ripen on the plant—they are much loved by wildlife.

Floral barrel

Edible flowers such as pot marigolds (*Calendula*) and nasturtiums (*Tropaeolum*) add a flamboyant touch to salads and other dishes, and they also look dazzling together in a large container. They are all easy to grow and will help to bring in pollinators such as bees and butterflies as well as beneficial insects such as ladybeetles, lacewings, and hoverflies. Pot marigolds and nasturtiums may draw aphids away from beans, so nestle this pot among your other crops. The wooden half-barrel gives the whole planting a rustic air.

Grow your own annual flowers by sowing seed of pot marigolds (see p162), sunflowers (*Helianthus*) (see p163), and nasturtiums (see p167) early in spring and placing them on a warm windowsill until they are ready to go out into the half-barrel. Alternatively you can buy all these plants as transplants from garden centers or by mail order. As lavender (*Lavandula*, see p166) rarely comes true from seed, it is easier to buy pot-grown plants when your annuals are ready for their final pot. English lavender (for example, *L. angustifolia* or *L.* x *intermedia*) can cope better with wet potting soil over winter in colder climates than French types (*L. stoechas*), which need lots of grit added to the potting mix for good drainage. The deeper purple-flowered varieties look best among the brightly colored annuals in this combination.

Place the barrel in a sunny spot—good light and warmth will ensure lots of flowers and help to generate the essential oils that give lavender its beautiful fragrance. All these plants like free-draining soil, so add a generous layer of drainage material to the bottom of the barrel before planting. Stake the sunflowers if they need it and pinch back the growing tips of the nasturtiums to strengthen the plants and encourage bushier growth. Once the annuals have all died back, cut back the flowering spikes on the lavender. Give it a further trim every year during early spring.

It is hard to believe that this striking pot is full of edible flowers, yet each of these plants will brighten a salad or add another dimension to a variety of meals.

Planting your floral barrel

What you need

- pot marigold, nasturtium, and sunflower seed, or young plants; ■ small pots for growing on; ■ half-barrel; ■ drainage material (see p15); ■ soil-based potting mix; ■ 2 x English lavender such as *Lavandula angustifolia* 'Munstead'

1 Sow nasturtiums and pot marigolds in small pots of potting soil and keep them moist on a sunny windowsill. Thin out the seedlings once they have their true leaves. Pot up until they are large enough to go outside. Sow sunflowers individually in three pots and grow on the same way.

2 Line the base of the half-barrel with drainage material and then top up to about two thirds full with potting mix, leaving enough room for planting and easy watering. Plant three sunflowers in the center of the half-barrel, then position the nasturtiums so that they will cascade over the edge.

3 Plant the lavenders, and fill in-between with pot marigold plants. Firm the potting soil around the rootballs. Then water all the plants well. Throughout summer water regularly so the plants do not dry out. Give them a liquid 5–5–10 feed every two weeks.

4 Harvest the edible leaves and flowers of nasturtium regularly and pick the sunflower petals when the flowers open. Gather the pot marigolds and lavender when needed. Keep on harvesting or deadheading the flowers to encourage more to come.

5 Add color and zing to a salad by sprinkling through some freshly picked nasturtium flowers and leaves. Both have a peppery taste similar to watercress and will liven up any summer meal.

Dwarf, clump-forming varieties of daylilies are perfect for growing in pots.

French lavender (*L. stoechas*) must have free-draining potting soil—that is its best winter protection.

Daylily

Daylilies (*Hemerocallis*) produce masses of flowers, each lasting only a single day, hence their common name. With regular picking they flower continuously all summer.

Basic needs
All parts of daylily, which are popular in Chinese food, are edible: the small buds can be eaten like beans; the unopened flowers are lovely in tempura; and the petals can be scattered on salads and soups. These tough perennials are easy to grow, doing best in a large pot or tub 8in. (20cm) or more deep. Use soil-based potting mix for stability, because most plants are tall, or select dwarf varieties such as 'Cranberry Baby.' Plant in spring or the fall in full sun, although plants with darker flowers prefer some shade. For constant flowers keep the potting mix moist and deadhead as soon as flowers have gone over.

Harvesting and storage
Cut the whole plant down in late fall and divide plants every three years to prevent them from becoming congested and rootbound.

Lavender

Lavender (*Lavandula*) is a hugely popular flower, long used medicinally as a soother and relaxant, and it is now increasingly fashionable as an edible flower in cookies, bread, or teas. There are hundreds of different types, and all look good in terra-cotta pots 8in. (20cm) or more deep.

Basic needs
For the best flower scent plant lavender in a sunny spot (see p164), although it does tolerate some shade. Plant in spring or fall in light, free-draining potting mix, then water. Do not overwater this Mediterranean plant, nor let it sit with wet feet, especially at night. Keep soil almost dry in colder months and protect plants against harsh winters. Give plants a close trim in spring, but do not cut back into old wood. Keep picking and deadheading flowers. Look out for rosemary beetle and its larvae, which feed on the leaves; shake them onto newspaper and destroy.

Harvesting and storage
Pick flowers just as they open and use fresh or hang up bunches for drying.

The much loved nasturtium is almost perfect in every way—beautiful, edible, and beneficial to the environment.

Deadhead and pinch back violas regularly to stop plants getting drawn and leggy.

Nasturtium

Another edible favorite is nasturtium (*Tropaeolum*). Its flowers, leaves, and even the seed pods are all eaten for their sweet, peppery taste. They are delicious in salads or when battered and fried, and each part of nasturtium tastes as lovely as it looks.

Basic needs

Nasturtiums thrive in containers, hanging baskets, or window boxes filled with well-drained potting mix, so work in plenty of grit. Sow seed as soon as temperatures are warm in spring (see p165) and keep plants well watered. Most will climb if you offer support, or crawl over the side of the pot if you do not. Nasturtiums are also useful companion plants (see p27), said to attract blackfly away from fava beans and cabbages, and to encourage hoverflies, which attack aphids.

Harvesting and storage

The flowers are good only when used fresh, so pick them just before eating. Harvest seed pods while they are still green. Gather the leaves when you want them for a peppery punch in a salad.

Viola

The much-loved viola has a sweet, fragrant flavor that is quite unlike the peppery punch of many other edible flowers. Violets (*Viola odorata*) have a pungent sweetness, while other types such as heartsease (*V. tricolor*) impart a lettuce- or pealike taste. Use the flowers in salads, desserts, and teas. In flower for a large part of the year violas could not be easier or more rewarding to cultivate in your yard.

Basic needs

Buy transplants, available from the fall onward; or sow in spring by simply pushing the seed into the potting mix. Leave the seed uncovered while it germinates. Violas are easy, unfussy plants and grow just about anywhere. They thrive in full sun, in any container, window box, or hanging basket 4in. (10cm) or more deep. Keep deadheading plants for a continuous supply of flowers all through the growing season.

Harvesting and storage

Gather flowers from spring until early winter for use fresh, dried, or crystallized for later enjoyment.

Spring in your step

Sometimes you just cannot wait to get started because there is nothing more exciting than the first harvest of the year. This simple pot contains a selection of crops that can all be sown and harvested within a few short weeks in spring.

Speedy growers, which also make useful catch or intercrops (see p16), are ideal ingredients for their own dedicated window box. Start off the container in midspring, using light, free-draining potting mix and place it in a warm, sunny place. There is no need to feed these first crops because they are growing for such a short time and most potting soil has sufficient nutrients to last the few weeks that these plants are in growth. Water and weed them carefully, particularly during hot weather because spinach and lettuce will struggle to germinate if the weather is too warm and will also bolt before you know it. Move the trough somewhere cool if the temperatures really heat up and keep harvesting the leaves, radishes, and scallions when young. Pick and deadhead the viola flowers.

All of these crops could easily be sown continuously throughout the growing season for a constant supply. By switching to hardier varieties as the summer progresses this trough could take you right through to the following year. If you do extend the harvest, fork in a sprinkling of slow-release fertilizer when resowing, to give later crops extra nutrients. If the viola plants get tired, replace with fresh ones.

Above: This simple, pretty pot will keep you in edible viola flowers for fresh salads throughout the year. They should last a long time if picked over often enough.

Left: Harvest crops as and when they are ready. Pull the scallions and radishes before they get too big and gather the spinach leaves and cut-and-come-again lettuce leaves whenever you need them.

Planting your spring pot

What you need

- trough or window box 18in. (45cm) or more in length;
- drainage material (see p15);
- all-purpose potting mix;
- 3 x viola plants;
- sand for marking out;
- lettuce, spinach, scallion, and radish seed.

1 Line the bottom of the trough with drainage material and then cover with potting soil until the trough is three quarters full. Evenly space the viola plants on the surface of the potting soil and then plant them, filling in with more potting soil. Water well.

2 Use sand to mark out where the vegetables are to go, sprinkling fine lines onto the surface of the potting soil. If you do not like the look of the design you can simply rub out the sand with your fingers and mark it out again.

3 When you are happy with the design for your trough, sow each vegetable seed into the sand. Then draw the surrounding potting soil over the seed until it is at the sowing depth recommended on the relevant seed packet. Water well.

4 Most of these seedlings should take only a week or so to germinate. When they are big enough to handle, thin them out carefully to give them room to grow. Remove any weeds since they will compete with the crops for water and nutrients.

5 Keep watering your trough. Radishes in particular can split if they do not grow steadily, and spinach bolts if conditions get too dry. Harvest the radishes when they are young and crisp, pulling them gently from the potting soil. Crop the other vegetables when needed.

Glossary

All-purpose soilless mix A *potting mix* made from peat, loam, sand, and bark plus some lime and fertilizers so it is suitable for sowing and growing a wide range of plants. Peat-free all-purpose soilless mixes are also available.

Annual A plant that completes its life cycle—germinating, flowering, and dying—in one year.

Bareroot A plant with no, or very little, soil on its roots when purchased.

Biennial A plant that completes its life cycle in two years.

Bolt/run to seed To produce seeds prematurely, usually after rapid flowering. Is generally caused by hot, dry, or sudden cold weather.

Catch crop Fast-growing plants that are sown and grown in the interval between harvesting a *maincrop* and sowing or planting another.

Cordon A *tree* or *shrub* trained as a single stem, and often supported against a wall with wires.

Cross-pollination/cross-fertilization The transfer of pollen from the stamens of one flower to the stigma of a flower on another plant.

Cultivar A contraction of cultivated variety, or cv. Refers to a plant that originated in cultivation rather than in the wild. Is often used interchangeably with the term *variety*.

Deadheading The removal of dead or fading flowers to prevent them from going to seed. This is done to promote further flowering, and to tidy up the plant.

Dibble A hand tool used to make sowing or planting holes.

Dieback [n] The death of a stem or other part of a plant after localized damage or infection. Often seen as discolored patches on the stem and wilting leaves. Needs to be pruned out so symptoms do not spread.

Ericaceous Term describing any plant that needs acidic soil (with a pH of 6.5 or less): for example, blueberries. Also refers to the type of acidic-soil mix that these plants need to grow in.

Espalier A *tree* or *shrub* with a vertical trunk and horizontal stems, often trained against a wall.

Fan A *tree* or *shrub* trained so that the branches radiate out in one plane from a single, short stem.

Furrow (as in seed furrow) A straight, narrow, shallow trench or line in which seeds are sown.

Garden compost Homemade organic material formed by spent plant material mixed with paper, cardboard, and some kitchen waste; this is left to break down into a humus-rich, dark compost. Is generally used for mulching and feeding the soil.

Genus A category in plant classification used to describe a group of closely related plants ranked between family and *species*.

Grow bag A commercial plastic bag specifically filled with nutrient-enriched *potting mix* and used for growing crops, instead of planting them in a pot or the open ground.

Half-barrel A recycled container made from a wooden barrel that has been cut in half.

Heritage variety/heirloom variety Old, often rare, varieties that taste delicious or have an unusual color or shape, and grow well on a garden scale. They are generally open pollinated, which means they are nonhybrid and have never been genetically modified. Growers can therefore save their seed for use in future years.

Intercrop Fast-growing crops such as radishes that are sown between rows of other slower-maturing crops such as parsnips, thereby making maximum use of growing space. The intercrop is harvested before the slower crops are fully grown.

Maincrop (of vegetables) Those cultivars that produce crops during the main growing season. Maincrop potatoes are usually harvested from midsummer onward. They also take slightly longer than early-season ones to mature, and they are larger potatoes, taking up more room. They store well, unlike other potato types.

Manure Well-rotted organic material added to soil or *garden compost* to increase fertility. Is usually of animal origin.

Minarette A freestanding *cordon*, trained as a single, vertical stem.

Misting, hand Term describing the spraying of plants with a fine mist of water to increase the humidity in the air around them. Is often done to combat pests, such as red spider mite.

Mulch A layer of organic or inorganic material that sits on the surface of the soil or potting mix and reduces moisture loss, acts as a barrier against weeds and pests, prevents compaction, and helps to insulate plant roots against cold weather.

Perennial A plant that lives for more than two years.

Potting mix A medium for growing plants. There are many different types including *all-purpose*, *soil-based*, *soilless*, and acidic-soil mix. All include different constituents depending on the types of plants for which they are required.

Potting up Term describing the transplanting of seedlings or young plants into larger pots to give them room to keep growing.

Repotting Term describing the process of planting a container-grown plant into a new pot the same size, after reducing its rootball slightly to make room for some fresh *potting mix*.

Rootbound Term describing a plant that has outgrown its pot and its roots have become restricted, causing the plant to grow poorly.

Rootstock The lower section of a grafted plant, which controls the size the plant will grow to. It is joined to the *scion*.

Run to seed *see Bolt*.

Scion A shoot or bud that is cut from one plant to graft onto a *rootstock*. The scion is the upper section of the plant.

Seed drill *see Furrow*.

Shrub A plant that has woody stems from or near the base but no central trunk.

Soil-based potting mix A *potting mix* made from a mixture of soil, peat, and sand with added nutrients. Soil-based potting mix is best for large pots, since it is heavy and stable, and is suitable for thirsty plants, because it holds moisture well. It is often better for longer-term planting.

Soilless potting mix A *potting mix*, usually based on peat rather than soil, but sometimes of coconut or bark. Contains varying amounts of nutrients, depending on the use for the soilless potting mix: for example, seeds need fewer nutrients than longer-term plants. Is excellent for small pots, window boxes, and baskets because of its light weight.

Species A category in plant classification used to describe a group of closely related plants ranked between a *genus* and *variety*. Such plants come *true* to type from seed.

Spot sowing To sow individually or in groups of two or three seeds at fixed intervals in a pot or *furrow*. This is a good way to sow economically and it reduces the need to thin later—just nip off the weakest seedling after germination.

Spur bearer A fruit *tree* that carries its fruit in clusters on short branches known as spurs. These take two years to form.

Standard/half-standard A *tree* or *shrub* grown with a single, clear stem up to 6½ft. (2m). A half-standard is the same but shorter, being around 5ft. (1.5m) tall.

Taproot The long, primary anchoring root of some plants that grows vertically downward: for example, on a parsnip or cilantro plant.

Tip bearer A fruit *tree* that carries its fruit mainly on the ends of shoots produced the previous year.

Topdressing Term describing the application of a layer of fresh *potting mix* to the surface of a container to replenish nutrients; it is usually done after removing the top layer of old potting mix. Also refers to the decorative *mulch* applied to the soil surface around a plant.

Tree A plant with a central, woody trunk or stem.

True/true-breeding Term describing a plant that gives rise to offspring similar to the parent when self pollinated; *species* plants come true from seed unlike F_1 hybrids.

Variety A category in plant classification used to describe a group of closely related plants ranked below that of *species*. Is often used more familiarly and interchangeably with *cultivar*.

Index

Acknowledgments

The publishers would like to thank the following suppliers who have helped to make this book by generously supplying their products and time:

For cans, potting mixes, fertilizer, nets and pots:

Julia Leakey at Crocus www.crocus.co.uk;

Sophie Hedges at Garden Trading www.gardentrading.co.uk;

Victoria Myhill at Harrod Horticultural www.harrodhorticultural.com;

Andrew at Hen & Hammock www.henandhammock.co.uk;

Emma De Maio at Stewarts www.stewartcompany.co.uk;

Nicola Bacon at Westland Horticulture www.gardenhealth.com and Marshalls Seeds www.marshalls-seeds.co.uk;

Heather Gorringe and Sandra Montague at Wiggly Wigglers www.wigglywigglers.co.uk.

For seed and young plants:

David Turner at Mr Fothergill's www.mr-fothergills.co.uk;

Sally Norman at Sarah Raven www.sarahraven.com;

Francijn Suermondt and Shaun Brazendale at Suttons Seeds www.suttons.co.uk;

Julie Butler at Thompson & Morgan www.thompson-morgan.com;

For helping us to photograph their pots:

Matthew Wilson, Victoria Kyme, Lucy Roberts and Charlotte Muswell at Clifton Nurseries www.clifton.co.uk; Mario De Pace at R.H.S. Garden Wisley www.rhs.org.uk; Jenny Richmond; Teresa Farnham; Don Mapp; Chris Achilleos at Marsh Lane Allotments; Mark Ridsill Smith; and Andy Male.

Photography credits

(t) top, (b) bottom, (l) left, (m) middle, (r) right

All photos by Steven Wooster except:

GAP Photos: 59 bm Zara Napier.

Garden World Images: 95 G.W.I./ Flowerphotos/J.Buckley; 124 r J.Swithinbank.

Octopus Publishing Group: David Sarton 10–11, 14 tr, 123 b Gabriel Ash/R.H.S. Chelsea Flower Show 2008; 24 l; 83 t; 130 l; 131. Torie Chugg 23 m; 42 t; 47; 48 l & r; 71 b; 71 tl. Stephen Robson (from Creative Vegetable Gardening) 68.

Suttons Seeds: 88 t; 118 b; 119; 123 t; 129 r; 157 t; 166 l.

The Garden Collection: 19 Liz Eddison/Design by Philippa Pearson/R.H.S. Hampton Court; 25 tr Neil Sutherland; 35 t Bob Kennett-F.L.P.A.; 96 Derek St. Romaine.

Thinkstock: Dorling Kindersley RF 20 t; 31 b; 70; 76 b; 100 l; 114 t; 134 l & r; 153 b. Goodshoot 74–75. Hemera 26 bl; 34 l; 42 b; 51; 69; 76 t; 85 br; 114 b; 160–161; 163 l; 166 r. iStockphoto 8 l & r; 13 l; 14 tl & tr; 16; 18; 20 b; 23 t; 24 r; 26 br; 29 br; 30 l & r; 32; 34 r; 35 b; 40–41; 45 br; 46; 49; 50; 52 t & b; 53; 56 t & b; 57 t & b; 59 br; 61; 63 br; 64 l, m & r; 67 br; 72 r; 77 r; 82; 87 br; 88 b; 92; 93 b; 97 b; 100 r; 101; 107 l & r; 108; 109 t & b; 112 b; 113; 118 t; 122; 128 t; 130 r; 135 t & b; 138–139; 140 t & b; 141 t; 142; 143 r; 148 b; 149 ml & bl; 153 t; 156; 157 b; 162 l; 163 r; 165 br. Zoonar 65, 162 r, 167 l.